Ecce Romani

A Latin Reading Program
Revised Edition

2

Rome at Last

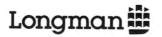
Longman

Ecce Romani Student's Book 2   Rome at Last

Copyright © 1984 by Longman. All rights reserved. No part of this book or related recordings may be reproduced, stored in a retrieval system, or transmitted in any form or means, electronic, mechanical, photocopying, recording, or otherwise, without prior permission from the publisher.

First Printing 1984

ISBN 0 582 36665 8
(72459)

Illustrated by Peter Dennis, Trevor Parkin, Hamish Gordon and Claudia Karabaic Sargent. Cover illustration by Peter Dennis.

This edition of *Ecce Romani* is based on *Ecce Romani: A Latin Reading Course*, originally prepared by The Scottish Classics Group © copyright The Scottish Classics Group 1971, 1982, and published in the United Kingdom by Oliver and Boyd, a Division of Longman Group. This edition has been prepared by a team of American and Canadian educators:
  Authors: Professor Gilbert Lawall, University of Massachusetts, Amherst,
               Massachusetts
               David Tafe, Rye Country Day School, Rye, New York
  Consultants: Dr. Rudolph Masciantonio, Philadelphia Public Schools, Pennsylvania
               Ronald Palma, Holland Hall School, Tulsa, Oklahoma
               Dr. Edward Barnes, C.W. Jefferys Secondary School, Downsview,
               Ontario
               Shirley Lowe, Wayland Public Schools, Wayland, Massachusetts

For providing us with photographs or permission to publish extracts from their publications, we would like to thank:
Page 62: The Montreal Museum of Fine Arts, photograph of Roman Magistrates and Lictors by Jean Lemaire, French 1598-1659, oil on canvas. A gift of Lord Strathcona and family.
Page 58: Harvard University Press, publisher of Loeb Classical Library, Pliny *Natural History*, Volume X Book XXXVI-XXXVII, copyright © 1962 by the President and Fellows of Harvard College.
Pages 21, 47, and 91: Carol Clemeau Esler, *Roman Voices: Everyday Latin in Ancient Rome* and *Teacher's Guide to Roman Voices: Everyday Latin in Ancient Rome*, published by Gilbert Lawall, 71 Sand Hill Road, Amherst, MA 01002.

Longman, 10 Bank Street, White Plains, N.Y. 10606

Distributed in Canada by Academic Press Ltd., 55 Barber Greene Road, Don Mills, Ontario MC3 2A1, Canada.

10-MU-95949392

CONTENTS

17
Arrival at the Inn

Raeda in fossā haerēbat. Cornēliī per viam ībant ad caupōnam quae nōn procul aberat. Cornēlia, quae nōn iam lacrimābat, cum Eucleide ambulābat. Puerōs, quod praecurrēbant, identidem revocābat Cornēlius. Aurēlia, quamquam in caupōnā pernoctāre adhūc nōlēbat, lentē cum Cornēliō ībat. Mox ad caupōnam appropinquābant. Nēminem vidēbant; vōcēs tamen hominum audiēbant. 5

Subitō duo canēs ē iānuā caupōnae sē praecipitant et ferōciter lātrantēs Cornēliōs petunt. Statim fugit Sextus. Stat immōbilis Marcus. Aurēlia perterrita exclāmat. Cornēlius ipse nihil facit. Cornēlia tamen nōn fugit sed ad canēs manum extendit. 10

"Ecce, Marce!" inquit. "Hī canēs lātrant modo. Nūllum est perīculum. Ecce, Sexte! Caudās movent."

Eō ipsō tempore ad iānuam caupōnae appāruit homō obēsus quī canēs revocāvit.

"Salvēte, hospitēs!" inquit. "In caupōnā meā pernoctāre vultis? Hīc multī 15 cīvēs praeclārī pernoctāvērunt. Ōlim hīc pernoctāvit etiam lēgātus prīncipis."

"Salvē, mī Apollodōre!" interpellāvit Eucleidēs. "Quid agis?"

"Mehercule!" respondit caupō. "Nisi errō, meum amīcum Eucleidem agnōscō."

"Nōn errās," inquit Eucleidēs. "Laetus tē videō. Quod raeda dominī meī 20 in fossā haeret immōbilis, necesse est hīc in caupōnā pernoctāre."

"Doleō," inquit caupō, "quod raeda est in fossā, sed gaudeō quod ad meam caupōnam nunc venītis. Intrāte, intrāte, omnēs!"

praecurrō, praecurrere (3), to run ahead	**revocāvit,** (he) called back
homō, hominis (*m*), man	**hospes, hospitis** (*m*), friend, host, guest
sē praecipitant, (they) hurl themselves, rush	**pernoctāvērunt,** (they) have spent the night
fugiō, fugere (3), to flee	**ōlim,** once (upon a time)
manum, hand	**lēgātus, -ī** (*m*), envoy
hī canēs, these dogs	**Quid agis?** How are you?
modo, only	**Mehercule!** By Hercules! Goodness me!
cauda, -ae (*f*), tail	**nisi errō,** unless I am mistaken
appāruit, (he) appeared	**agnōscō, agnōscere** (3), to recognize
obēsus, -a, -um, fat	**doleō, dolēre** (2), to be sad

5

Exercise 17a

Respondē Latīnē:

1. Quō ībant Cornēliī?
2. Cūr Cornēlius puerōs identidem revocābat?
3. Volēbatne Aurēlia in caupōnā pernoctāre?
4. Quid canēs faciunt?
5. Quālis homō ad iānuam caupōnae appāruit?
6. Quālēs cīvēs in caupōnā pernoctāvērunt?
7. Quis ōlim in caupōnā pernoctāvit?
8. Cūr necesse est in caupōnā pernoctāre?
9. Gaudetne caupō quod raeda est in fossā?

Exercise 17b

Using story 17 as a guide, give the Latin for:

1. The inn was not far away.
2. Cornelius kept calling the boys back.
3. Aurelia was unwilling to spend the night in the inn.
4. Two dogs head for the boys.
5. The two dogs are wagging their tails.
6. I am glad to see you.
7. The innkeeper is sorry that the coach is in the ditch.

Cavē canem! *Beware of the dog!* (Pompeian inscription)

Errāre est hūmānum. *To err is human.* (Seneca)

Manus manum lavat. *One hand washes the other.*
   (Petronius, *Satyricon* 45)

Regular Verbs

Most Latin verbs belong to one of four conjugations:

THE PRESENT TENSE						
		1st Conjugation	*2nd* Conjugation	*3rd* Conjugation		*4th* Conjugation
Infinitive		par*āre*	hab*ēre*	mitt*ere*	iac*ere* (*-iō*)	aud*īre*
Imperative		par*ā*	hab*ē*	mitt*e*	iac*e*	aud*ī*
		par*āte*	hab*ēte*	mitt*ite*	iac*ite*	aud*īte*
Number and Person — *Singular*	1	par*ō*	habe*ō*	mitt*ō*	iaci*ō*	audi*ō*
	2	par*ās*	hab*ēs*	mitt*is*	iac*is*	aud*īs*
	3	para*t*	habe*t*	mitti*t*	iaci*t*	audi*t*
Plural	1	par*āmus*	hab*ēmus*	mitt*imus*	iac*imus*	aud*īmus*
	2	par*ātis*	hab*ētis*	mitt*itis*	iaci*tis*	aud*ītis*
	3	para*nt*	habe*nt*	mittu*nt*	iaciu*nt*	audiu*nt*

THE IMPERFECT TENSE						
		1st Conjugation	*2nd* Conjugation	*3rd* Conjugation		*4th* Conjugation
Number and Person — *Singular*	1	parā*bam*	habē*bam*	mittē*bam*	iaciē*bam*	audiē*bam*
	2	parā*bās*	habē*bās*	mittē*bās*	iaciē*bās*	audiē*bās*
	3	parā*bat*	habē*bat*	mittē*bat*	iaciē*bat*	audiē*bat*
Plural	1	parā*bāmus*	habē*bāmus*	mittē*bāmus*	iaciē*bāmus*	audiē*bāmus*
	2	parā*bātis*	habē*bātis*	mittē*bātis*	iaciē*bātis*	audiē*bātis*
	3	parā*bant*	habē*bant*	mittē*bant*	iaciē*bant*	audiē*bant*

Be sure you know all of these forms thoroughly.

Irregular Verbs

A few verbs do not belong to any of the four conjugations shown on the previous page, but you will notice that, except for the forms **sum** and **possum**, they have the same personal endings as the regular verbs.

		THE PRESENT TENSE					
Infinitive		esse	posse	velle	nōlle	īre	ferre
Imperative		es	—	—	nōlī	ī	fer
		este	—	—	nōlīte	īte	ferte
Number and Person — Singular	1	sum	possum	volō	nōlō	eō	ferō
	2	es	potes	vīs	nōn vīs	īs	fers
	3	est	potest	vult	nōn vult	it	fert
Plural	1	sumus	possumus	volumus	nōlumus	īmus	ferimus
	2	estis	potestis	vultis	nōn vultis	ītis	fertis
	3	sunt	possunt	volunt	nōlunt	eunt	ferunt

		THE IMPERFECT TENSE					
Number and Person — Singular	1	eram	poteram	volēbam	nōlēbam	ībam	ferēbam
	2	erās	poterās	volēbās	nōlēbās	ībās	ferēbās
	3	erat	poterat	volēbat	nōlēbat	ībat	ferēbat
Plural	1	erāmus	poterāmus	volēbāmus	nōlēbāmus	ībāmus	ferēbāmus
	2	erātis	poterātis	volēbātis	nōlēbātis	ībātis	ferēbātis
	3	erant	poterant	volēbant	nōlēbant	ībant	ferēbant

Be sure to learn these forms thoroughly.

Exercise 17c

Read and translate the following short sentences, paying particular attention to the tenses of the verbs:

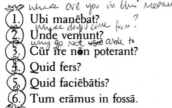

1. Ubi manēbat?
2. Unde veniunt?
3. Cūr īre nōn poterant?
4. Quid fers?
5. Quid faciēbātis?
6. Tum erāmus in fossā.
7. Quō īre volunt?
8. Quid respondēbant?
9. Cūr praecurrēbant?
10. Quid facere iubēbat?
11. Nōn poteram clāmāre.
12. Quō ītis?

8

13. Quid ferēbās?
14. Quid facitis?
15. Quid vidēs?
16. Ubi haeret raeda?
17. In viā pernoctāre nōlumus.
18. Quō ībant?
19. Ad urbem īre nōn vult.

20. Unde veniēbās?
21. Scelestī estis.
22. Quō equōs dūcit?
23. Quō fugiēbant?
24. Cūr īre nōlunt?
25. Caupōna nōn procul aberat.
26. Manēre nōlēbāmus.

Unde . . . ? Where . . . from?

Adjectives

Some adjectives have endings like those of 1st and 2nd declension nouns, and others have 3rd declension endings, as shown in the following chart:

Number Case	1st and 2nd Declension			3rd Declension		
	Masc.	*Fem.*	*Neut.*	*Masc.*	*Fem.*	*Neut.*
Singular						
Nom.	magn*us*	magn*a*	magn*um*	omn*is*	omn*is*	omn*e*
Gen.	magn*ī*	magn*ae*	magn*ī*	omn*is*	omn*is*	omn*is*
Acc.	magn*um*	magn*am*	magn*um*	omn*em*	omn*em*	omn*e*
Abl.	magn*ō*	magn*ā*	magn*ō*	omn*ī*	omn*ī*	omn*ī*
Plural						
Nom.	magn*ī*	magn*ae*	magn*a*	omn*ēs*	omn*ēs*	omn*ia*
Gen.	magn*ōrum*	magn*ārum*	magn*ōrum*	omn*ium*	omn*ium*	omn*ium*
Acc.	magn*ōs*	magn*ās*	magn*a*	omn*ēs*	omn*ēs*	omn*ia*
Abl.	magn*īs*	magn*īs*	magn*īs*	omn*ibus*	omn*ibus*	omn*ibus*

Be sure to learn these forms thoroughly.

Notes

1. Some adjectives that have endings of the 1st and 2nd declensions end in **-er** in the masculine nominative singular, e.g., **miser.** The feminine and neuter of this adjective are **misera** and **miserum.** In some words, the **-e-** is dropped from all forms except the masculine nominative singular, e.g., **noster, nostra, nostrum; nostrī, nostrae, nostrī.** Compare with the noun **ager, agrī** (*m*).

2. Many adjectives of the 3rd declension have identical forms in the masculine and feminine, as does **omnis** above.

3. The ablative singular of 3rd declension adjectives ends in **-ī** (not **-e**), and the genitive plural ends in **-ium.** The neuter nominative and accusative plurals end in **-ia.** Compare these endings with those of 3rd declension nouns that you learned in Chapters 11 and 15.

9

Agreement of Adjectives

The gender, case, and number of an adjective are determined by the noun with which it *agrees*. Consider the following sentence:

Multōs agrōs, multās arborēs, multa plaustra vident.

Since **agrōs** is a masculine noun in the accusative plural, **multōs** has a masculine accusative plural ending. Similarly, **multās** is feminine accusative plural *agreeing* with **arborēs**, and **multa** is neuter accusative plural *agreeing* with **plaustra**. An adjective will *agree* with the noun it describes in *gender, case*, and *number*.

There are five clues which help you to decide with which noun an adjective agrees. These are *gender, case, number, sense*, and *position*.

1. Let us look at the first three clues (agreement of gender, case, and number):

   a. Sometimes any one of the three *agreement* clues will show which noun an adjective modifies:

      Māter bonōs puerōs laudat.
      The mother praises the good boys.

      Māter and **puerōs** are different in gender, case, and number, and therefore all the clues in **bonōs** are decisive.

   b. Sometimes only two of these clues are present:

      Māter bonās puellās laudat.
      The mother praises the good girls.

      In this sentence **māter** and **puellās** have the same gender, but either of the two other clues (case and number) will help.

   c. In the following sentences only one of the *agreement* clues is present:

      Māter bonam puellam laudat.
      The mother praises the good girl.

      Since **māter** and **puellam** have the same gender and number, only the case of **bonam** is decisive.

      Mātrem bonum puerum laudāre iubēmus.
      We order the mother to praise the good boy.

      Here, it is the gender alone which is decisive.

      Mātrem bonās puellās laudāre iubēmus.
      We order the mother to praise the good girls.

      Here, only the number is decisive.

10

2. You will find examples where none of the clues of agreement will help you. When this happens, you must rely on position or sense:

> **Puellam ignāvam epistulam scrībere iubēmus.**
> *We order the lazy girl to write the letter.*

3. Note that either adjectives that take 1st and 2nd declension endings or adjectives of the 3rd declension may be used with nouns of any declension, as is shown in the following phrases:

māter bona	**omnium puellārum**
patrem bonum	**omnēs puerī**
iter bonum	**omnī puerō**
itinerī bonō	**omnī itinere**
itinera bona	**omnia itinera**

The important thing is that the adjective must *agree* with the noun it modifies in *gender, case,* and *number.*

Exercise 17d

In the following sentences, the most important clues to meaning are those of agreement of adjectives. Sometimes words appear in an unusual order with adjectives separated from the nouns they modify.

Read aloud and translate:

1. Canis magnus ossa habet.
2. Canis magna ossa habet.
3. Multī canēs ossa habent.
4. Canis magnum os habet.
5. Omnia ossa magnus canis habet.
6. Magna habent multī canēs ossa.
7. Magnum canis habet os.
8. Omnēs canēs dominōs nōn habent.
9. Magnum habet dominus canem.
10. Canem dominus magnum habet.
11. Habent multī puerī magnōs canēs.
12. Magnōs multī habent puerī canēs.

> **os, ossis** (*n*), bone

> **Nōn omnia possumus omnēs.** *We cannot all do everything.*
> (Vergil, *Eclogues* VIII.63)

Versiculī: *"Arrival at the Inn," page 99.*

Word Study V

Latin Suffixes -(i)tūdō *and* -(i)tās

A Latin adjective may form a noun by adding the suffix -(i)tūdō or the suffix -(i)tās to its base. The base of a Latin adjective may be found by dropping the ending from the genitive singular, e.g., the base of **magnus** (genitive, **magnī**) is **magn-**. Nouns formed in this way are in the 3rd declension, they are feminine, and they convey the meaning of the adjective in noun form.

Adjective			Base	Noun
Nom.	*Gen.*			
magnus	magnī	big, great	magn-	magnitūdō, magnitūdinis (*f*) size, greatness
obēsus	obēsī	fat	obēs-	obēsitās, obēsitātis (*f*) fatness

In English words derived from these nouns, -(i)tūdō becomes -(i)tude and -(i)tās becomes -(i)ty. The meaning of the English derivative is usually the same as that of the Latin noun, e.g., *magnitude* (size), *obesity* (fatness).

Exercise 1

Give the Latin nouns which may be formed from the bases of the adjectives below. In numbers 1–4, use the suffix -(i)tūdō, and in numbers 5–10, use the suffix -(i)tās. Give the English word derived from each noun formed, and give the meaning of the English word.

1. sōlus, -a, -um
2. multus, -a, -um
3. longus, -a, -um
4. sollicitus, -a, -um
5. ūnus, -a, -um

6. brevis, -is, -e
7. īnfirmus, -a, -um
8. timidus, -a, -um
9. vīcīnus, -a, -um
10. hūmānus, -a, -um

Latin Suffixes -īlis, -ālis, -ārius

The suffixes -īlis, -ālis, and -ārius may be added to the bases of many Latin nouns to form adjectives. The base of a Latin noun may be found by dropping the ending from the genitive singular, e.g., the base of vōx (genitive, vōcis) is vōc-. Adjectives formed in this way mean "pertaining to" the meaning of the noun from which they are formed.

Noun		Base		Adjective
Nom.	Gen.			
vir	virī	man	vir-	virīlis, -is, -e manly
vōx	vōcis	voice	vōc-	vōcālis, -is, -e pertaining to the voice
statua	statuae	statue	statu-	statuārius, -a, -um pertaining to statues

Some adjectives ending in -ārius are used as nouns, e.g., statuārius, -ī (m), sculptor. Can you think of similar words made from the nouns raeda, -ae (f), coach, and tabella, -ae (f), tablet, document?

English words derived from these adjectives make the following changes in the suffixes:

-īlis becomes -il or -ile, e.g., virīlis, virile
-ālis becomes -al, e.g., vōcālis, vocal
-ārius becomes -ary, e.g., statuārius, statuary

The meaning of the English derivative is similar to or the same as that of the Latin adjective, e.g., virīlis in Latin and virile in English both mean "manly." Sometimes the English word ending in -ary may be used as a noun, e.g., statuary, "a group or collection of statues," "sculptor," or "the art of sculpting."

Exercise 2

For each English word below, give the following:

a. the Latin adjective from which it is derived
b. the Latin noun from which the adjective is formed
c. the meaning of the English word.

You may need to consult a Latin and/or English dictionary for this exercise.

auxiliary	principal
civil	puerile
literary	servile
nominal	temporal

Combining Suffixes

Some English words end with a combination of suffixes derived from Latin. For example, the English word *principality* (domain of a prince) is derived from the Latin **prīnceps, prīncipis** (*m*) by the combination of the suffixes -**ālis** (-*al* in English) and -**itās** (-*ity* in English).

Exercise 3

For each word below, give the related English noun ending in the suffix -*ity*. Give the meaning of the English word thus formed and give the Latin word from which it is derived.

civil	immobile
dual	partial
facile	servile
hospital	virile

English Replaced by Latin Derivatives

In the following exercise, the italicized English words are not derived from Latin. Note that these words are usually simpler and more familiar than the Latin derivatives which replace them. Latin can help with the meanings of many of these more difficult English words.

Exercise 4

Replace the italicized words with words of equivalent meaning chosen from the pool on page 15. Use the Latin words in parentheses to determine the meanings of the English words in the pool.

1. Staying at an inn was much too *risky* for Aurelia. perilous
2. While he was away, Cornelius left the children in the *guardianship* of Eucleides. custody
3. Although the driver *handled* the reins skillfully, he was unable to avoid disaster. manipulated
4. It was *easy to see* that Eucleides was a friend of the innkeeper. apparent
5. The *runaway* slave was captured and returned to the farm. fugitive
6. The innkeeper offered his *friendly welcome* to the Cornelii. hospitality
7. The heat made the slaves' work more *burdensome*. onerous
8. The Via Appia is full of *traveling* merchants, who sell their wares from town to town. itinerant
9. Cornelia cast a *sorrowful* glance as she waved goodbye to Flavia. doleful
10. This *country* inn was host to all the local farmers. rustic

custody (**custōs**)	hospitality (**hospes**)
itinerant (**iter**)	fugitive (**fugere**)
apparent (**appārēre**)	perilous (**perīculum**)
doleful (**dolēre**)	onerous (**onus**)
manipulated (**manus**)	rustic (**rūsticus**)

Latin Words in English

Some Latin words are used in English in their Latin form. Many of these words have become so familiar in English that they are pluralized using English rules, e.g.:

senator	plural: *senators*
area	plural: *areas*

Others retain their Latin plurals, e.g.:

alumnus	plural: *alumni*
alumna	plural: *alumnae*
medium	plural: *media*

Sometimes both an English and a Latin plural are used, e.g.:

index	plurals: *indexes, indices*
memorandum	plurals: *memorandums, memoranda*

Occasionally the use of two plurals may reflect more than one meaning of the word. For example, the word *indexes* usually refers to reference listings in a book, whereas *indices* are signs or indicators, e.g., "the indices of economic recovery."

Exercise 5

Look up these nouns in both an English and a Latin dictionary. For each noun, report to the class on similarities or differences between the current meaning in English and the original meaning in Latin. Be sure to note carefully the English plurals and their pronunciation.

antenna	consensus	formula
appendix	crux	stadium
campus	focus	stimulus

18
Settling In

Cūnctī in caupōnam intrāvērunt.

"Nōnne cēnāre vultis?" inquit caupō. "Servī meī bonam cēnam vōbīs statim parāre possunt."

"Ego et Cornēlia," inquit Aurēlia, "hīc cēnāre nōn possumus. Dūc nōs statim ad cubiculum nostrum." 5

Servōs caupō statim iussit cēnam Cornēliō et Marcō et Sextō parāre. Ipse Aurēliam et Cornēliam ad cubiculum dūxit. Aurēlia, ubi lectum vīdit, gemuit.

"Hic lectus est sordidus," inquit. "Mea Cornēlia in sordidō lectō dormīre nōn potest. Necesse est alium lectum in cubiculum movēre." 10

Caupō respondit, "Cūr mē reprehendis? Multī viātōrēs ad meam caupōnam venīre solent. Nēmō meam caupōnam reprehendit."

Iam advēnit Eucleidēs. Ubi Aurēlia rem explicāvit, Eucleidēs quoque caupōnem reprehendit.

Caupō mussāvit, "Prope viam Appiam caupōnam meliōrem invenīre nōn 15 potestis. In caupōnā meā nūllī lectī sunt sordidī."

Sed servōs iussit alium lectum petere. Brevī tempore servī alium lectum in cubiculum portāvērunt. Caupō iam cum rīsū clāmāvit, "Ecce, domina! Servī meī alium lectum tibi parāvērunt. Nōnne nunc cēnāre vultis?"

"Ego nōn iam ēsuriō," inquit Cornēlia. "Volō tantum cubitum īre." 20

"Ego quoque," inquit Aurēlia, "sum valdē dēfessa."

Nōn cēnāvērunt Aurēlia et Cornēlia, sed cubitum statim īvērunt. Mox dormiēbant.

---

intrāvērunt, (they) entered
cēnō, cēnāre (1), to dine, eat dinner
cēna, -ae (f), dinner
vōbīs, for you
Dūc! Take! Lead!
iussit, (he) ordered
Cornēliō, for Cornelius
dūxit, (he) led
lectus, -ī (m), bed
hic lectus, this bed
sordidus, -a, -um, dirty

viātor, viātōris (m), traveler
venīre solent, (they) are in the habit of coming
rem explicāre, to explain the situation
melior, better
tibi, for you
ēsuriō, ēsurīre (4), to be hungry
cubitum īre, to go to bed
valdē, very, exceedingly, very much
īvērunt, they went

Exercise 18a

Respondē Latīnē:

1. Quid servī caupōnis parāre possunt?
2. Vultne Aurēlia statim cēnāre?
3. Quid fēcit Aurēlia ubi lectum vīdit?
4. Quālis est lectus?
5. Quid fēcit Eucleidēs ubi Aurēlia rem explicāvit?
6. Quid servī in cubiculum portāvērunt?
7. Cūr Cornēlia cēnāre nōn vult?
8. Quid fēcērunt Aurēlia et Cornēlia?

> Quid fēcit . . . ? What did . . . do?

VERBS: Perfect Tense I

Compare the following pairs of sentences:

Caupō **mussat**.	*The innkeeper* **mutters**.
Caupō **mussāvit**.	*The innkeeper* **muttered**.
Dāvus servōs **iubet** canēs dūcere.	*Davus* **orders** *the slaves to lead the dogs.*
Caupō servōs **iussit** cēnam parāre.	*The innkeeper* **ordered** *the slaves to prepare dinner.*
Marcus **gemit**.	*Marcus* **groans**.
Aurēlia **gemuit**.	*Aurelia* **groaned**.
Marcus nūntium in vīllam **dūcit**.	*Marcus* **leads** *the messenger into the house.*
Cornēliam ad cubiculum **dūxit**.	*He* **led** *Cornelia to the bedroom.*
Cornēlius vōcēs hominum **audit**.	*Cornelius* **hears** *men's voices.*
Cornēlius vōcēs hominum **audīvit**.	*Cornelius* **heard** *men's voices.*

In each of the pairs of examples listed above, the verb in the first example is in the present tense and the verb in the second example is in the *perfect tense.*

The perfect tense refers, not to something that *is happening* (present tense) or *was happening* (imperfect tense), but to something that *happened* in the past (see examples above). It may also refer to something that *has happened*, e.g.:

Servus meus alium lectum tibi **parāvit**.	*My slave* **has prepared** *another bed for you.*

or to something that *did* or *did* not *happen*, e.g.:

Aurēlia nōn **cēnāvit**.	*Aurelia* **did** *not* **eat dinner**.

17

In the perfect tense, the ending of the 3rd person singular is **-it**; the ending of the 3rd person plural is **-ērunt**.

In many verbs, the stem for the perfect tense ends in **-v-** or **-s-** or **-u-** or **-x-**, e.g.:

mussāv-   iuss-   gemu-   dūx-   audīv-

The perfect endings are then added to the perfect stem, e.g.:

mussāv*it*   iuss*it*   gemu*it*   dūx*it*   audīv*it*
mussāv*ērunt*   iuss*ērunt*   gemu*ērunt*   dūx*ērunt*   audīv*ērunt*

Here are some more examples:

Singular		Plural	
Present	*Perfect*	*Present*	*Perfect*
exclāmat	exclāmāvit	exclāmant	exclāmāvērunt
habet	habuit	habent	habuērunt
rīdet	rīsit	rīdent	rīsērunt
cōnspicit	cōnspexit	cōnspiciunt	cōnspexērunt

Exercise 18b

Give the missing forms and meanings to complete the following table:

Perfect Tense		Infinitive	Meaning
Singular	*Plural*		
intrāvit	intrāvērunt	intrāre	to enter
_____	custōdīvērunt	_____	_____
timuit	_____	_____	_____
_____	cēnāvērunt	_____	_____
_____	traxērunt	_____	_____
mīsit	_____	_____	_____
_____	īvērunt	_____	_____
spectāvit	_____	_____	_____
doluit	_____	_____	_____
_____	mānsērunt	_____	_____
_____	voluērunt	_____	_____
haesit	_____	_____	_____

18

Exercise 18c

Read the following passage and answer the questions in full Latin sentences:

Cornēliī per viam ad caupōnam lentē ambulābant.
Sextus, "Nōnne ille tabellārius equōs vehementer incitāvit, Marce?"
Cui respondit Marcus, "Ita vērō! Eōs ferōciter verberāvit. Equī cisium
celeriter traxērunt. Raedārius noster, 'Cavē, sceleste!' magnā vōce exclāmāvit.
Tum raedam dēvertēbat, sed frūstrā. Tabellārius tamen neque cisium dēvertit   5
neque raedam vītāvit. Itaque equī raedam in fossam traxērunt. Gemuit raedārius; gemuērunt pater et māter; lacrimāvit Cornēlia."
    "Pater tuus certē īrātus erat," interpellāvit Sextus. "Statim virgam arripuit
et miserum raedārium verberābat. Cornēlia, ubi hoc vīdit, iterum lacrimāvit.
'Pater! Pater!' inquit. 'Nōlī miserum hominem verberāre!'"   10
    "Tum pater," inquit Marcus. "Cornēliam tacēre iussit. Omnēs sollicitī
caelum spectāvērunt quod iam advesperāscēbat. Pater igitur Eucleidem nōs
ad caupōnam dūcere iussit."
    Mox caupōnam cōnspexērunt. Intrāvērunt Cornēliī et brevī tempore cē-
nāvērunt.   15

> vehementer incitāre, to drive hard
> cui, to whom, to him, to her
> certē, certainly
> arripuit, he seized
> hoc, this

1. What did the driver shout?
2. Where did the horses drag the coach?
3. What did Cornelius and Aurelia do when the coach went into the ditch?
4. What did Cornelia do?
5. What did Cornelius seize?
6. What did Cornelia say when Cornelius beat the coachman?
7. What did Cornelius order Cornelia to do?
8. What did Cornelius do when he saw that it was getting dark?

Exercise 18d

Read aloud and translate:

Dum Cornēliī ad caupōnam lentē ībant, raedārius equōs custōdiēbat. Miser erat quod Cornēlium timēbat. Mox adveniunt duo servī caupōnis.

"Salvē!" inquiunt. "Quid accidit? Quid faciēbās? Raedamne ferōciter agē-bās? Cūr nōn dīligenter viam spectābās? Dormiēbāsne?"

Sed raedārius miser, "Minimē vērō!" respondet. "Raedam magnā arte 5 agēbam. Puerī mē vexābant; tacēre nōlēbant. Ego certē nōn dormiēbam. Sed cūr vōs adestis? Vultisne mē adiuvāre? Potestisne raedam ex fossā extrahere?"

Tum omnēs diū labōrābant, sed raedam neque servī neque equī extrahere poterant. Tandem dēfessī ad caupōnam redeunt.

"Raedam movēre nōn poterāmus," inquiunt. "Necesse est magnum nu- 10 merum servōrum mittere."

accidit, (it) happened   **adsum, adesse** (*irreg.*), to be present
dīligenter, carefully   **adiuvō, adiuvāre** (1), to help

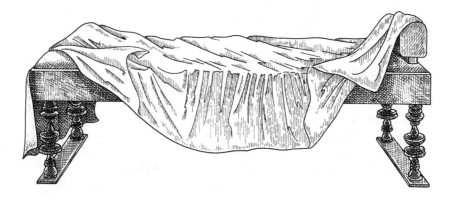

Bed reconstructed from fragments in the
National Roman Museum.

Graffiti from Ancient Inns

I

Assibus hīc bibitur; dīpundium sī dederis, meliōra bibēs;
quattus sī dederis, vīna Falerna bibēs.

A drink is had here for one as; if you pay two, you'll drink better (wines);
if you pay four, you'll drink Falernian.

II

Viātor, audī. Sī libet, intus venī: tabula est aēna quae tē cūncta
perdocet.

Traveler, listen. Come inside if you like: there's a bronze tablet which
gives you all the information.

III

Tālia tē fallant utinam mendācia, caupō:
tū vēndis aquam et bibis ipse merum.

I hope these deceptions get you into trouble, innkeeper:
you sell water and drink the pure wine yourself.

IV

Mīximus in lectō. Fateor, peccāvimus, hospes.
Sī dīcēs, "Quārē?" Nūlla matella fuit.

I wet the bed. I have sinned, I confess it, O host.
If you ask why: there was no chamber-pot.

V

"Caupō, computēmus."
"Habēs vīnī (sextārium) I, pānem a. I, pulmentār. a. II."
"Convenit."
"Puell. a. VIII.'
"Et hoc convenit."
"Faenum mūlō a. II."
"Iste mūlus mē ad factum dabit!"

"Innkeeper, let's reckon up (the bill)."
"You have 1 pint of wine, 1 as-worth of bread, 2 asses-worth of food."
"Right."
"Girl, 8 asses."
"That's right, too."
"Fodder for the mule, 2 asses."
"That darn mule is going to bankrupt me!"

21

Horace's Journey

This account of Horace's journey from Rome to Brundisium describes some of the hazards with which travelers might be faced:

After I had left great Rome, I put up in Aricia in a humble inn. My companion was Heliodorus, a teacher of rhetoric. From there we went to Forum Appii, a town packed with boatmen and grasping innkeepers. We were idle enough to take this part of the journey in two stages; for the more energetic it is only one; the Appian Way is less tiring for leisurely travelers. Here, because of the water, which is very bad, I suffered an upset stomach; and it was in a bad temper that I waited for my companions to finish their evening meal. As we were about to go on board, the boatmen began to argue. A whole hour went past while the fares were being collected and the mule harnessed. The vicious mosquitoes and marsh-frogs made sleep impossible while the boatman, who had drunk too much cheap wine, sang of his absent girlfriend, and a passenger joined in the singing.

At last the weary passengers fell asleep; and the idle boatman turned the mule out to graze, fastened its halter to a stone, and lay on his back snoring.

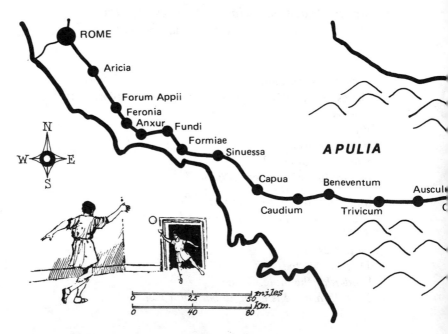

At dawn we realized we weren't moving. A hot-tempered passenger leapt up and beat the boatman and the mule with a stick. When at last we disembarked, it was almost ten o'clock. With due reverence and ceremony we washed our hands and faces in the fountain of Feronia. After lunch we "crawled" the three miles* to Anxur, which is perched on rocks that shine white in the distance. There our very good friend Maecenas was due to meet us. As my eyes were giving me trouble, I smeared black ointment on them. Meanwhile, Maecenas arrived with that perfect gentleman, Fonteius Capito. We were glad to leave Fundi behind, with its self-appointed "praetor" Aufidius Luscus. How we laughed at the official get-up of the ambition-crazy clerk, his toga praetexta and the tunic with the broad stripe. At last, tired out, we stayed in the city of Formiae, where Murena provided accommodation and Capito a meal.

The next day we reached Sinuessa and were met by Varius, Plotius, and Vergil—friends to whom I was most attached. Then a small villa next to the Campanian bridge gave us shelter; and the official purveyors, as they were obliged to do, provided us with wood and salt. After we left here, our pack-mules were unsaddled early at Capua. Maecenas went to play ball, Vergil and I to sleep; for ball games are bad for a man with sore eyes and an upset stomach. After Capua, Cocceius received us in a house with ample provisions built above the inns of Caudium.

* about two and three-fourths modern English miles or four and a half kilometers.

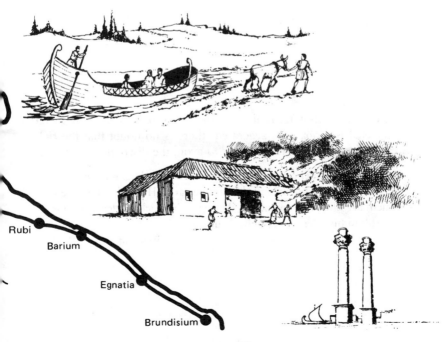

Rubi

Barium

Egnatia

Brundisium

From here we made our way right on to Beneventum, where the over-worked innkeeper nearly burned the place down while roasting lean thrushes on a spit. Soon after leaving Beneventum, I saw again the familiar mountains of my native Apulia. We would never have struggled over those mountains if we had not found lodgings at Trivicum. There the smoke made our eyes water, for they put green branches on the fire, leaves and all. There also I waited until midnight for a deceitful girl who never showed up. What a fool I was!

From here we sped on twenty-four miles * in carriages, intending to lodge in the small town of Ausculum. Here they charge for the cheapest of all commodities—water. The bread, however, is very good indeed, so that the experienced traveler usually takes some away in his bag; for the bread at Canusium is as hard as a stone, and the water supply is no better.

From here we arrived at Rubi, tired out—as was to be expected—for the stage was long and the road conditions difficult because of heavy rain. After this the weather was better, but the road worse as far as Barium, a fishing town. Then Egnatia provided us with laughter and amusement: the people tried to convince us that in the temple there frankincense melts without a flame. I don't believe it!

Brundisium is the end of my long account and of my long journey.

Horace, Satires I.5 (abridged)

* about 22 modern English miles or 36 kilometers.

Although the following account given by Cicero of how one provincial governor traveled is probably exaggerated, there is no doubt that the rich and powerful often went to great lengths to avoid the discomforts of travel:

Verres traveled in a litter carried by eight bearers. In the litter was a cushion of transparent Maltese linens stuffed with roseleaves. He held to his nose a close-mesh bag filled with rosepetals. Whenever he reached a town, he was carried, still in his litter, direct to his bedroom.

Cicero, in Verrem II.27

Travel by Land

Gaius Cornelius and his family traveled from Baiae to Rome along a section of the Via Appia, which ran south from Rome to Brundisium—a distance of 358 miles or 576 kilometers. It was part of a network of major highways that radiated from the Golden Milestone (**mīliārium aureum**), in the Forum at Rome, to all parts of the Empire. These roads, originally built by the legions to make easy movement of troops possible, were laid on carefully made foundations with drainage channels at both sides and were usually paved with slabs of basalt. Although travel was safer and easier than at any time before the "Railway Age," it was nevertheless extremely slow by modern standards. The **raeda** seldom averaged more than five miles or eight kilometers per hour; a man walking might manage twenty-five miles or forty kilometers a day; an imperial courier on urgent business might, with frequent changes of horse, manage to cover over 150 miles or 240 kilometers in twenty-four hours. Since carriage wheels had iron rims and vehicles lacked springs, a journey by road was bound to be uncomfortable. Moreover, since the vehicles were open or, at best, had only a canopy, the travelers often had to endure both clouds of dust and attacks from insects.

The following passage illustrates these discomforts:

> When I had to make my way back from Baiae to Naples, to avoid the experience of sailing a second time, I easily convinced myself that a storm was raging. The whole road was so deep in mud that I might as well have gone by sea. That day I had to endure what athletes put up with as a matter of course: after being anointed with mud, we were dusted with sand in the Naples tunnel. Nothing could be longer than that prison-like corridor, nothing dimmer than those torches that do not dispel the darkness but merely make us more aware of it. But even if there were light there, it would be blacked out by the dust which, however troublesome and disagreeable it may be in the open, is, as you can imagine, a thousand times worse in an enclosed space where there is no ventilation and the dust rises in one's face. These were the two entirely different discomforts which we suffered. On the same day and on the same road we struggled through both mud and dust.
>
> Seneca, *Epistulae Morales* LVII

25

19
Chance Encounter

Ubi Cornēlia et māter cubitum īvērunt, Marcus et Sextus cum Cornēliō mānsērunt. Cum Cornēliō cēnāre et post cēnam ad mediam noctem vigilāre in animō habuērunt, nam omnia vidēre et omnia audīre voluērunt.

Marcus, "Ēsuriō, pater," inquit. "Ēsurīsne tū quoque, Sexte?"

"Ita vērō!" respondit Sextus.   5

"Semper ēsurītis, tū et Marcus!" exclāmāvit Cornēlius.

"Licetne nōbīs," inquit Marcus, "hīc cēnāre?"

Paulīsper tacēbat pater, sed tandem, "Estō!" inquit. "Tibi et Sextō licet hīc cēnāre. Post cēnam tamen necesse est statim cubitum īre."

Rīsērunt puerī quod laetī erant. "Gaudēmus, pater," inquit Marcus, 10 "quod nōs in cubiculum nōn statim mīsistī. Voluimus enim hīc manēre et aliōs viātōrēs spectāre."

Tum Cornēlius caupōnem iussit cibum parāre. Brevī tempore servus cibum ad eōs portāvit. Dum puerī cibum dēvorant, subitō intrāvit mīles quīdam. Cornēlium attentē spectāvit. "Salvē, vir optime!" inquit. "Salvēte, 15 puerī! Cūr vōs in hanc caupōnam intrāvistis? Cūr nōn ad vīllam hospitis īvistis? Nōnne tū es senātor Rōmānus?"

"Senātor Rōmānus sum," respondit Cornēlius. "Nōs in hanc caupōnam intrāvimus quod raeda nostra in fossā haeret immōbilis. In agrīs nocte manēre nōlēbāmus, sed numquam anteā in caupōnā pernoctāvimus. Certē in agrīs 20 pernoctāre est perīculōsum."

Tum mīles, "Etiam in caupōnā pernoctāre saepe est perīculōsum."

"Cūr hoc nōbīs dīcis?" rogāvit Cornēlius. "Estne hic caupō homō scelestus? Dē Apollodōrō quid audīvistī?"

"Dē Apollodōrō nihil audīvī, sed semper est perīculōsum in caupōnā 25 pernoctāre. Vōsne audīvistis illam fābulam dē caupōne nārrātam? Ille caupō hospitem necāvit."

"Minimē!" inquit Cornēlius. "Illam fābulam nōn audīvī. Cūr igitur nōbīs illam nōn nārrās dum cēnāmus?"

mānsērunt, (they) stayed	**mīsistī,** you have sent
post (+ *acc.*), after	**voluimus,** we wanted
media nox, midnight	**enim,** for
vigilō, vigilāre (1), to stay awake	**mīles quīdam,** a certain soldier
in animō habēre, to intend	**mīles, mīlitis** (*m*), soldier
licet nōbīs, we are allowed, we may	**vir optime!** sir!
paulīsper, for a short time	**optimus, -a, -um,** best, very good
Estō! All right!	**in hanc caupōnam,** into this inn

numquam, never
anteā, before
dīcō, dīcere (3), to say
dē (+ *abl.*), about
audīvī, I have heard

illam fābulam dē caupōne nārrā-tam, that famous story told about the innkeeper
necō, necāre (1), to kill
nārrō, nārrāre (1), to tell (a story)

Exercise 19a

Respondē Latīnē:

1. Quid fēcērunt Marcus et Sextus ubi Cornēlia et Aurēlia cubitum īvērunt?
2. Quid puerī facere voluērunt?
3. Ēsuriuntne puerī?
4. Licetne Marcō et Sextō in caupōnā cēnāre?
5. Cūr puerī laetī sunt?
6. Quis intrāvit dum puerī cibum dēvorant?
7. Quid rogat?
8. Cūr Cornēlius in agrīs pernoctāre nōlēbat?
9. Quid mīles dē Apollodōrō audīvit?
10. Quid fēcit caupō in fābulā?

Exercise 19b

Using story 19 as a guide, give the Latin for:

1. Marcus and Sextus wished to stay awake until midnight.
2. Cornelius ordered the slave to bring food.
3. Soon a soldier entered and suddenly looked at Cornelius.
4. Cornelius said, "I came into this inn because my carriage is stuck in a ditch."
5. Cornelius has never before spent the night in an inn.
6. What has the soldier heard about Apollodorus?
7. Cornelius has not heard that famous story told about the innkeeper.

VERBS: Perfect Tense II

You have now met all the endings of the perfect tense.

	1	*-ī*		1	*-imus*
Singular	2	*-istī*	Plural	2	*-istis*
	3	*-it*		3	*-ērunt*

These are the endings of the perfect tense of *all* Latin verbs, e.g.:

	1	mīs*ī*		1	mīs*imus*
Singular	2	mīs*istī*	Plural	2	mīs*istis*
	3	mīs*it*		3	mīs*ērunt*

28

Exercise 19c

With proper attention to the new perfect tense endings, read aloud and translate:

1. Marcus et Sextus ad mediam noctem vigilāre in animō habuērunt.
2. Ego et tū cubitum īre nōluimus.
3. Mīlesne Cornēlium spectāvit?
4. Cūr voluistī hīc pernoctāre, Marce?
5. Cūr in caupōnā pernoctāvistis, puerī? Licetne fīliō senātōris in caupōnam intrāre?
6. Cornēlius in cubiculum servum īre iussit.
7. Puerī laetī fuērunt quod ad mediam noctem vigilāvērunt.
8. Dum Cornēlius et puerī cēnant, mīles fābulam nārrāvit.
9. Ego et Cornēlius in agrīs manēre timēbāmus.
10. Omnia vidēre et audīre volunt quod numquam anteā in caupōnā pernoctāvērunt.

> fuī, I was (perfect of sum)

Exercise 19d

Supply the appropriate perfect tense endings, read aloud, and translate:

1. Ego līberōs in hortō petīv_____; tū eōs in silvā invēn_____.
2. Ubi tunica Sextī in rāmīs haerēbat, nōs omnēs rīs_____.
3. Quō īvistī, Cornēlia? Ego et Marcus patrem hoc rogāv_____, sed ille nihil respond_____.
4. Quamquam Sextus fu_____ molestus, servī eum nōn verberāv_____.
5. Ubi herī fu_____, Marce et Cornēlia? Pater et māter nōs iuss_____ hīc manēre.
6. Postquam vōs cēnāv_____, cubitum īre volu_____.
7. Herī nōs ad urbem īv_____, sed mātrem ibi nōn vīd_____.
8. "Unde vēn_____, amīcī?" rogā_____ caupō. "Quō nunc ītis?"
9. Tūne Cornēlium vīd_____, ubi tū Rōmam advēn_____? Ego certē eum nōn vīd_____.
10. Ille, postquam hoc audīv_____, ē caupōnā sē praecipitāv_____.

> ille, he
> herī, yesterday
> postquam, after

Roman Hospitality

Because inns were dirty and often dangerous, well-to-do Romans tried to avoid staying in them. Instead, they tried to plan their journey so that they could stay at the **vīlla** of a **hospes**. This word means "host" or "guest," but it is also translated as "friend," although in this special sense it has no exact equivalent in English. It describes a relationship established between two families in the past and kept up by every succeeding generation. As a result of such a relationship, a traveler could go to the house of his "family friend"—whom in some cases he personally might never have met—and claim **hospitium** for the night, producing, if need be, some token such as a coin that had been halved as proof of the link between the two families. Members of the host's family, if they happened to be traveling in a district in which their guest's family owned a **vīlla,** could claim similar rights of hospitality. It could extend to other situations. For instance, if a Roman had business interests in one of the provinces, someone residing there might look after them for him. In return, he might have some service done for him in Rome. Cornelius, you may remember, is responsible for Sextus' education while his father is in Asia.

VERBS: Principal Parts

When we refer to a Latin verb, we normally give the four *principal parts*, from which all forms of that verb may be derived. These principal parts are:
  the 1st person singular of the present tense
  the present infinitive
  the 1st person singular of the perfect tense
  the supine.

	Present	Infinitive	Perfect	Supine	Meaning
1st Conj.	parō	parāre (1)	parāvī	parātum	to prepare
2nd Conj.	habeō	habēre (2)	habuī	habitum	to have
3rd Conj.	mittō	mittere (3)	mīsī	missum	to send
	iaciō	iacere (3)	iēcī	iactum	to throw
4th Conj.	audiō	audīre (4)	audīvī	audītum	to hear

Be sure to learn the above forms thoroughly.

Notes

1. The perfect stem is found by dropping the -ī from the end of the third principal part of the verb. The perfect endings are then added directly to this stem.

30

2. The principal parts of most verbs in the 1st, 2nd, and 4th conjugations follow the patterns on the opposite page. There is no set pattern for 3rd conjugation verbs.

3. In vocabulary lists from this point on, the verbs in the 1st, 2nd, and 4th conjugations which follow the set patterns will appear as follows:

> **clāmō** (1), to shout
> **appāreō** (2), to appear
> **pūniō** (4), to punish

When they do not follow the pattern, they will be given in full, e.g.:

> **lavō, lavāre** (1), **lāvī, lavātum,** to wash
> **veniō, venīre** (4), **vēnī, ventum,** to come

Third conjugation verbs will be given in full, e.g.:

> **dūcō, dūcere** (3), **dūxī, ductum,** to lead

Exercise 19e

Read aloud and translate each verb form given at the left below. Then deduce and give the first three principal parts for each verb:

	1st Sing. Present	Present Infinitive	1st Sing. Perfect
necāmus, necāvimus	necō	necāre (1)	necāvī
intrant, intrāvērunt			
errās, errāvistī			
tenēs, tenuistī			
mittunt, mīsērunt			
manēmus, mānsimus			
iubet, iussit			
discēdimus, discessimus			
haeret, haesit			
dormiunt, dormīvērunt			
petunt, petīvērunt			
custōdīmus, custōdīvimus			
gemitis, gemuistis			

Can you give the principal parts for the following?

estis, fuistis			

31

20
Murder

Mīles hanc fābulam nārrāvit.

Duo amīcī, Aulus et Septimus, dum iter in Graeciā faciunt, ad urbem Megaram vēnērunt. Aulus in caupōnā pernoctāvit, in vīllā hospitis Septimus. Mediā nocte, dum Septimus dormit, Aulus in somnō eī appāruit et clāmāvit, "Age, Septime! Fer mihi auxilium! Caupō mē necāre parat." 5

Septimus, somniō perterritus, statim surrēxit et, postquam animum recuperāvit, "Nihil malī," inquit. "Somnium modo fuit."

Deinde iterum obdormīvit. Iterum tamen in somnō Aulus suō amīcō appāruit; iterum Septimō clāmāvit, "Ubi ego auxilium petīvī, tū nōn vēnistī. Nēmō mē adiuvāre nunc potest. Caupō enim mē necāvit. Postquam hoc 10 fēcit, corpus meum in plaustrō posuit et stercus suprā coniēcit. In animō habet plaustrum ex urbe crās movēre. Necesse est igitur crās māne plaustrum petere et caupōnem pūnīre."

Iterum surrēxit Septimus. Prīmā lūce ad caupōnam īvit et plaustrum petīvit. Ubi plaustrum invēnit, stercus remōvit et corpus extrāxit. Septimus, 15 ubi amīcum mortuum vīdit, lacrimāvit. Caupō scelestus quoque lacrimāvit, nam innocentiam simulābat. Septimus tamen caupōnem statim accūsāvit. Mox cīvēs eum pūnīvērunt.

Postquam mīles fābulam fīnīvit, silentium fuit. Subitō Cornēlius exclāmāvit, "Agite, puerī! Nōnne vōs iussī post cēnam cubitum īre? Cūr ad 20 cubiculum nōn īvistis?"

Sed Marcus, "Pater, nōs quoque fābulam mīlitis audīre voluimus. Nōn dēfessī sumus. Nōn sērō est."

Hoc tamen dīxit Marcus quod cubitum īre timēbat. Dum enim fābulam mīlitis audiēbat, caupōnem spectābat. Cōgitābat, "Quam scelestus ille caupō 25 vidētur! Certē in animō habet mediā nocte mē necāre. Necesse est vigilāre."

Etiam Sextus timēbat. Cōgitābat tamen, "Sī hic caupō est scelestus, gaudeō quod mīles in caupōnā pernoctat. Eucleidēs certē nōs adiuvāre nōn potest."

Invītī tandem puerī cubitum īvērunt, vigilāre parātī. Mox tamen sēmi- 30 somnī fuērunt. Brevī tempore obdormīvit Marcus.

32

somnus, -ī (m), sleep
eī, to him
somnium, -ī (n), dream
animum recuperāre, to regain one's
  senses, be fully awake
Nihil malī. There is nothing wrong.
obdormiō (4), to go to sleep
corpus, corporis (n), body
stercus, stercoris (n), dung, manure

suprā, above, on top
prīmā lūce, at dawn
mortuus, -a, -um, dead
simulō (1), to pretend
fīniō (4), to finish
sērō, late
cōgitō (1), to think
vidētur, (he) seems
invītus, -a, -um, unwilling

surgō, surgere (3), surrēxī, surrēctum, to rise, get up
sum, esse (irreg.), fuī, to be
adiuvō, adiuvāre (1), adiūvī, adiūtum, to help
pōnō, pōnere (3), posuī, positum, to place, put
coniciō, conicere (3), coniēcī, coniectum, to throw
eō, īre, (irreg.), īvī, itum, to go
petō, petere (3), petīvī, petītum, to look for, seek
inveniō, invenīre (4), invēnī, inventum, to come upon, find
removeō, removēre (2), remōvī, remōtum, to remove
extrahō, extrahere (3), extrāxī, extractum, to drag out
videō, vidēre (2), vīdī, vīsum, to see
iubeō, iubēre (2), iussī, iussum, to order, bid
volō, velle (irreg.), voluī, to wish, want, be willing
dīcō, dīcere (3), dīxī, dictum, to say, tell

Exercise 20a

Respondē Latīnē:

1. Ubi est Megara?
2. Ubi pernoctāvit Aulus? Ubi erat amīcus Aulī?
3. Quandō Aulus Septimō appāruit?
4. Quid fēcit Septimus postquam animum recuperāvit?
5. Ubi caupō corpus Aulī posuit? Quid in animō habuit?
6. Quid Septimus prīmā lūce fēcit?
7. Quandō lacrimāvit Septimus?
8. Cūr lacrimāvit caupō?
9. Quid cīvēs fēcērunt?
10. Quid Marcus timēbat?
11. Quōmodo puerī cubitum īvērunt?
12. Quid Marcus et Sextus in animō habuērunt?

          Quandō. . . ? When. . . ?

Exercise 20b

The following sentences contain errors of fact in the light of the last story you read. Explain these errors and give new Latin sentences which correct them:

1. Duo puerī, Aulus et Septimus, urbem Rōmam intrāvērunt.
2. Aulus et Septimus frātrēs Marcī erant.
3. Septimus mediā nocte surrēxit quod ēsuriēbat.
4. Aulus auxilium petīvit quod lectus sordidus erat.
5. Cīvēs, postquam Septimum necāvērunt, corpus sub stercore cēlāvērunt.
6. Caupō Septimum accūsāvit postquam cīvem mortuum invēnit.
7. Septimus cīvēs pūnīre in animō habuit quod scelestī erant.
8. Cīvēs corpus in caupōnā sub lectō invēnērunt.
9. Marcus cubitum īre timuit quod silentium erat.
10. Cornēlius caupōnem pūnīvit quod Marcus eum accūsāvit.

Exercise 20c

Using the list of principal parts given in the vocabulary on page 33, give the Latin for:

1. What did you want, boys?
2. They got up suddenly.
3. The boys went to bed at last.
4. Septimus looked for the wagon.
5. What have you seen?
6. We went to the inn.
7. What did you say, Marcus?
8. We ordered Cornelia to go to sleep.
9. What have they found?
10. He placed the body in the wagon.

Vēnī, vīdī, vīcī. *I came, I saw, I conquered.* (Julius Caesar, after the battle of Zela, 47 B.C.; reported in Suetonius, *Julius Caesar* XXXVII)

Nihil sub sōle novum. *There's nothing new under the sun.* (Vulgate, *Ecclesiastes* I.10)

Mēns sāna in corpore sānō. *A sound mind in a sound body.* (Juvenal X.356)

VERBS: Perfect and Imperfect

The imperfect tense describes an action in the past which
a. went on for a time, or
b. was repeated, or
c. was beginning to happen.

The perfect tense describes an action in the past which *happened* or *was completed* on one occasion, e.g.:

Hoc **dīxit** Marcus quod cubitum īre **timēbat**.
Marcus **said** *this because he* **was afraid** *to go to bed.*

Virgam **arripuit** et raedārium **verberābat**.
He **grabbed** *the stick and* **beat** *the driver* repeatedly.

Cornēliī sollicitī caelum **spectāvērunt** quod iam **advesperāscēbat**.
The Cornelii **looked** *anxiously at the sky because it* **was** *already getting dark.*

Exercise 20d

Read aloud and translate, paying particular attention to the tenses of the verbs:

1. Marcus sub arbore sedēbat, sed subitō surrēxit.
2. Iam advesperāscēbat ubi viātōrēs aedificia urbis cōnspexērunt.
3. Caupōnam nōn intrāvimus quod ibi pernoctāre timēbāmus.
4. Caupō prope portam labōrābat ubi clāmōrem audīvit.
5. Ubi Aurēlia cubiculum intrāvit, Cornēlia adhūc dormiēbat.
6. "Tacēte, omnēs!" exclāmāvit Dāvus, nam dominus appropinquābat.
7. Postquam Aurēlia rem explicāvit, Eucleidēs quoque dolēbat.
8. Tū, Sexte, mox obdormīvistī, sed ego diū vigilābam.
9. Caupō mussābat quod servōs alium lectum petere iussistī.
10. Sextus caupōnam statim petīvit quod canēs lātrābant.

Quid hōc somniō dīcī potest dīvīnius? *What can be said to be more divinely inspired than this dream?* (Cicero, *On Divination* I.57, after telling the story of Aulus and Septimus)

Versiculī: *"Murder," page 99.*

Review IV

Exercise IVa

Supply Latin nouns or adjectives to match the English cues. Be sure to give the correct endings. Read each sentence aloud and translate it.

1. Puellae _____ ad cubiculum īvērunt, quod dormīre nōlēbant. (unwilling)
2. Multī servī _____ lectōs ē cubiculīs portāvērunt. (all)
3. Corpora _____ amīcōrum _____ _____ vīdimus. (of all) (our dead)
4. Servī scelestī _____ _____ in plaustrō posuērunt. (all the bodies)
5. Cīvis caupōnem _____ necāvit. (fat)
6. Lectī _____ sunt in _____ caupōnā. (dirty) (every)
7. Caupō fābulam dē _____ scelestō nārrāvit. (innkeeper)
8. Mīles longam fābulam dē _____ _____ nārrāvit. (all the innkeepers)
9. Corpus hominis _____ in plaustrō posuimus. (dead)
10. In _____ caupōnam prope urbem intrāvistis. (every)

Exercise IVb

Identify the tense, person, and number of each of the following verb forms. Then give the principal parts of the verb:

	Tense	Person	Number
1. veniēbātis	___	___	___
2. cōgitāvistis	___	___	___
3. coniciēbam	___	___	___
4. iussērunt	___	___	___
5. surrēxī	___	___	___
6. removēbās	___	___	___
7. clāmāvistī	___	___	___
8. obdormiēbāmus	___	___	___

Exercise IVc

Give the requested forms of the following verbs in the present, imperfect, and perfect tenses:

	Present	Imperfect	Perfect
1. dīcere (2nd sing.)	_____	_____	_____
2. īre (3rd pl.)	_____	_____	_____
3. appārēre (1st pl.)	_____	_____	_____
4. iacere (1st sing.)	_____	_____	_____
5. lavāre (3rd sing.)	_____	_____	_____
6. pūnīre (2nd pl.)	_____	_____	_____

Exercise IVd

Give the imperatives of the following verbs:

	Singular	Plural
1. īre	_____	_____
2. pōnere	_____	_____
3. ferre	_____	_____
4. explicāre	_____	_____
5. nōlle	_____	_____
6. esse	_____	_____
7. dolēre	_____	_____
8. venīre	_____	_____

Exercise IVe

Change the following verbs to the present tense and the perfect tense where requested. Keep the same person and number.

	Present	Perfect
1. poterat	_____	
2. volēbam	_____	_____
3. ferēbās	_____	
4. erāmus	_____	_____
5. nōlēbās	_____	_____
6. ībant	_____	_____
7. volēbātis	_____	_____
8. erās	_____	_____
9. ferēbātis	_____	
10. nōlēbat	_____	_____

Exercise IVf

Read aloud and translate:

Sextus tamen nōn obdormīvit, nam dē mīlitis fābulā cōgitābat. Itaque diū vigilābat et dē Aulō mortuō cōgitābat. Tandem, "Marce!" inquit. "Tūne timuistī ubi illam fābulam audīvistī?"

Sed Marcus nihil respondit. Iterum, "Marce!" inquit. "Tūne caupōnem spectābās?" Iterum silentium! Deinde Sextus, iam timidus, "Marce! Marce!" 5 inquit. "Cūr tū obdormīvistī? Cūr tū nōn vigilāvistī?"

Subitō sonitum in cubiculō audīvit Sextus. "Ō mē miserum! Audīvitne sonitum Aulus ille miser ubi caupō eum necāre parābat? Quālis sonitus fuit?"

Sonitum Sextus iterum audīvit. "Ō Eucleidēs!" inquit. "Cūr ad cubiculum nōndum vēnistī? Ō pater! Ō māter! Cūr mē in Italiam mīsistis? Voluistisne 10 ita mē ad mortem mittere? In Asiam ego redīre volō. Ibi enim nūllum est perīculum, sed perīculōsum est hīc in Italiā habitāre."

Multa sē rogābat Sextus, nam, quamquam puer temerārius esse solēbat, nunc mediā nocte sōlus in cubiculō tremēbat.

Itaque Sextus, per tōtam noctem vigilāre parātus, diū ibi sedēbat. "Quō- 15 modo iam ē manibus caupōnis scelestī effugere possum? Suntne omnēs cau- pōnēs scelestī? Fortasse caupō mē, filium cīvis praeclārī, necāre in animō habet. Quamquam Aulus aurum habuit, ego tamen nihil habeō, neque aurum neque pecūniam."

Ita cōgitābat Sextus. Iterum sonitum audīvit. Timēbat sed tandem surrēxit 20 invītus, nam omnēs cubiculī partēs īnspicere volēbat. Mox tamen rīsit. Ecce! Sub lectō erat fēlēs, obēsa et sēmisomna. Prope fēlem Sextus mūrem mortuum vīdit. Mussāvit Sextus, "Nōn necesse est hoc corpus sub stercore cēlāre!"

sonitum, sound	**ē manibus,** from the hands
ita, in this way	**aurum, -ī** (*n*), gold
mors, mortis (*f*), death	**pecūnia, -ae** (*f*), money
sē rogābat, (he) asked	**fēlēs, fēlis** (*f*), cat
himself, wondered	**mūs, mūris** (*m*), mouse
tōtus, -a, -um, whole	

tremō, tremere (3), **tremuī,** to tremble
īnspiciō, īnspicere (3), **īnspexī, īnspectum,** to examine

Exercise IVg

In the above passage, locate the following in sequence:

1. All verbs in the present tense.
2. All verbs in the imperfect tense.

3. All verbs in the perfect tense.
4. All infinitives.

Eavesdropping

It was quite dark. Cornelia was still wide awake. All kinds of exciting sounds were floating up from the inn downstairs, inviting her to go down and have a look. She slipped out of bed, put a shawl around her shoulders, and tiptoed into the corridor where Eucleides was on guard.

"Take me downstairs, Eucleides," she wheedled. "I've never seen the inside of an inn before." This was quite true, because a Roman away from home preferred to stay in a friend's villa and avoided inns if possible.

Eucleides took a lot of persuading, but Cornelia could always get around him; he soon found himself downstairs, looking into the main room, with Cornelia peering from behind his arm.

It was pretty dark inside, despite the lamps. The atmosphere was thick with smoke and reeked of garlic. On the far side Cornelia could see her father; and nearer were other customers seated on stools at rough tables, and an evil-looking group they were.

"Stay away from them, Cornelia," whispered Eucleides. "Those rogues would murder their own mothers for a silver **dēnārius.**

But Eucleides needn't have worried because they were all absorbed in what was going on at the far end of the low room, where a girl was dancing. Above the hum of conversation her singing could be heard to the accompaniment of a rhythmic clacking noise she seemed to be making with her fingers. "Makes that noise with castanets," whispered Eucleides. "Dancing girl from Spain, probably Gades."

But one person was not paying much attention to the entertainment— the **tabellārius,** whose reckless driving had ditched them. He had not come out of the incident unscathed. One of his horses had gone lame, and he was making the most of the enforced delay, drinking the innkeeper's best Falernian.

As Cornelia and Eucleides entered, the innkeeper was bringing forward a young man to introduce him to the imperial courier. "This is Decimus Junius Juvenalis, Sir, a soldier like yourself." The **tabellārius,** unbending slightly as a rather haggard young man came forward wearing the insignia of a junior officer, dismissed the innkeeper with a look and said pleasantly enough, "Greetings, young man! Where are you from?"

"I'm on my way back from service in Britain, sir. What a place! They don't have any climate there, just bad weather! Mist, rain, hail, snow—the lot! Hardly a blink of sunshine!"

"Perhaps he knows our Davus," whispered Cornelia.

"Let me see!" said the **tabellārius.** "Who's governor of Britain these days? A chap called Agricola, I hear."

"That's right!" replied Juvenalis. "A madman, if you ask me. He's not content with conquering the bit of Britain that's near Gaul, where you can get something profitable, like silver or wool or hides or those huge hunting dogs. Before I left he had gone to the very edge of the world where the Caledonii live. They say that there, in the middle of winter, the sun doesn't shine at all! But I can't vouch for that myself!"

"I've been to Britain too," said the **tabellārius,** much interested. "I'm not an ordinary **tabellārius,** you know. I'm really in charge of a section of the **cursus pūblicus.** I personally carry dispatches only if they are confidential messages from—"

And here he whispered something in Juvenalis' ear which Cornelia could not catch.

The innkeeper sidled up again with some more wine.

"We get lots of interesting people stopping here on the Via Appia," he confided. "Not only military gentlemen like yourselves, or that scum of humanity there"—jerking his thumb towards the dancer's audience—"but special envoys to the Emperor himself. When Nero was Emperor, we had one of this new Jewish religious sect who lodged here on a journey all the way from Judaea, to be tried by the Emperor himself no less! He was called Paul or something—"

Suddenly Cornelia felt her ear seized between finger and thumb and looked around into the eyes of a very angry Aurelia. She found herself upstairs and back in bed before she knew what had happened.

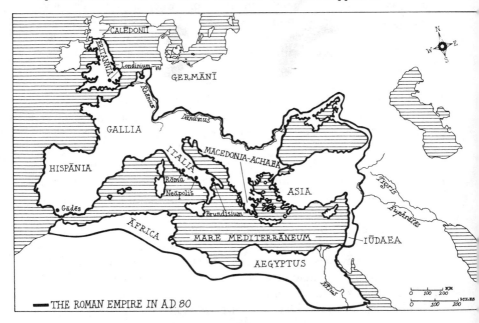

THE ROMAN EMPIRE IN A.D 80

21
From the Inn to Rome

Iam diēs erat. Prīmā lūce raedārius auxiliō servōrum caupōnis raedam ē
fossā extrāxit et ad caupōnam admōvit. Tum servī cistās Cornēliōrum raedāriō trādidērunt. Intereā in caupōnā, dum omnēs sē parābant, Sextus, iam
immemor terrōris nocturnī, mīlitis fābulam Cornēliae nārrābat; Eucleidēs
mandāta servīs dabat. Cornēlius ipse Aurēliae et līberīs clāmābat, "Agite, 5
omnēs! Nōlīte cessāre! Tempus est discēdere."

Tandem cūnctī ē caupōnā vēnērunt et in raedam ascendērunt.

"Valē!" clāmāvērunt puerī.

"Valēte!" respondit caupō, quī in viā stābat. "Nōlīte in fossam iterum
cadere! Nōn in omnibus caupōnīs bene dormīre potestis." 10

Tum raedārius habēnās sūmpsit et equōs verberāvit. Tandem Rōmam
iterum petēbant.

In itinere Sextus omnia dē mūre mortuō Marcō explicāvit, Cornēlius
mīlitis fābulam uxōrī nārrāvit. Iam urbī appropinquābant, cum subitō puerī
ingēns aedificium cōnspexērunt. 15

Marcus patrem, "Quid est illud?" rogāvit.

Atque Sextus, "Quis in illō aedificiō habitat?"

Cui Cornēlius, "Nēmō ibi habitat," cum rīsū respondit. "Est sepulcrum
Messallae Corvīnī quī erat ōrātor praeclārus. Hīc sunt sepulcra multōrum
et praeclārōrum cīvium quod Rōmānīs nōn licet intrā urbem sepulcra 20
habēre."

Mox alterum aedificium magnum vīdērunt.

"Estne id quoque sepulcrum, pater?" rogāvit Marcus.

"Ita vērō!" Cornēlius respondit. "Est sepulcrum Caeciliae Metellae. Nōnne
dē Caeciliā Metellā audīvistī?" 25

Sed Marcus patrī nihil respondit. Iam enim urbem ipsam vidēre poterat.
"Ecce Rōma!" clāmāvit.

"Ecce Rōma! Ecce Rōma!" clāmāvērunt Sextus et Cornēlia.

Tum Cornēlius, "Brevī tempore ad Portam Capēnam adveniēmus et
Titum, patruum vestrum, ibi vidēbimus. Epistulam enim per servum mīsī 30
et omnia eī explicāvī. Titus mox nōs prope Portam excipiet."

auxiliō, with the help
raedāriō, to the coachman
sē parāre, to prepare oneself, get ready
immemor, immemoris, forgetful
nocturnus, -a, -um, during the night
Cornēliae, to Cornelia
mandātum, -ī (n), order, instruction
bene, well
habēnae, -ārum (f pl), reins
mūs, mūris (m), mouse
uxōrī, to his wife

cum, when
ingēns, ingentis, huge
illud, that
atque, and
sepulcrum, -ī (n), tomb
intrā (+ acc.), inside
adveniēmus, we will come
patruus, -ī (m), uncle
vester, vestra, vestrum, your (pl)
vidēbimus, we will see
excipiet, (he) will welcome

admoveō, admovēre (2), admōvī, admōtum, to move towards
trādō, trādere (3), trādidī, trāditum, to hand over
dō, dare (1), dedī, datum, to give (note short a)
ascendō, ascendere (3), ascendī, ascēnsum, to climb
respondeō, respondēre (2), respondī, respōnsum, to reply
cadō, cadere (3), cecidī, cāsum, to fall
sūmō, sūmere (3), sūmpsī, sūmptum, to take, take up
cōnspiciō, cōnspicere (3), cōnspexī, cōnspectum, to catch sight of
excipiō, excipere (3), excēpī, exceptum, to welcome, receive

NOUNS: Cases and Declensions

Dative Case

Look at the following sentences:

1. Fābulam **Cornēliae** nārrābat. *He was telling a story to Cornelia.*
2. Omnia **Marcō** explicāvit. *He explained everything to Marcus.*
3. Mandāta **servīs** dabat. *He was giving orders to the slaves.*
4. Marcus **patrī** nihil respondit. *Marcus made no reply to his father.*
5. Aulus **eī** appāruit. *Aulus appeared to him.*
6. Lectum **tibi** parāvērunt. *They have prepared a bed for you.*

The Latin words in bold type are all in the *dative case.*

Amīcus omnibus amīcus nēminī. A *friend to everyone is a friend to no one.*

42

Here is a table showing the groups of nouns and cases, including the dative.

Number Case	1st Declension Fem.	2nd Declension Masc.	2nd Declension Masc.	2nd Declension Neut.	3rd Declension Masc.	3rd Declension Fem.	3rd Declension Neut.
Singular							
Nom.	puella	servus	puer	baculum	pater	vōx	nōmen
Gen.	puellae	servī	puerī	baculī	patris	vōcis	nōminis
Dat.	puellae	servō	puerō	baculō	patrī	vōcī	nōminī
Acc.	puellam	servum	puerum	baculum	patrem	vōcem	nōmen
Abl.	puellā	servō	puerō	baculō	patre	vōce	nōmine
Plural							
Nom.	puellae	servī	puerī	bacula	patrēs	vōcēs	nōmina
Gen.	puellārum	servōrum	puerōrum	baculōrum	patrum	vōcum	nōminum
Dat.	puellīs	servīs	puerīs	baculīs	patribus	vōcibus	nōminibus
Acc.	puellās	servōs	puerōs	bacula	patrēs	vōcēs	nōmina
Abl.	puellīs	servīs	puerīs	baculīs	patribus	vōcibus	nōminibus

Notes

1. In each declension dative and ablative plurals have the same endings.

2. The datives of the pronouns are as follows:

Singular		Plural	
Nominative	*Dative*	*Nominative*	*Dative*
ego	**mihi**	nōs	**nōbīs**
tū	**tibi**	vōs	**vōbīs**
is, ea, id	**eī**	eī, eae, ea	**eīs**

The dative endings of the adjectives are:

	1st and 2nd Declension			3rd Declension		
	Masc.	*Fem.*	*Neut.*	*Masc.*	*Fem.*	*Neut.*
Singular	magnō	magnae	magnō	omnī	omnī	omnī
Plural	magnīs	magnīs	magnīs	omnibus	omnibus	omnibus

Be sure to learn the new dative forms thoroughly.

Exercise 21a

Translate the following sentence:

Cornēlius fābulam uxōrī nārrāvit.

Now reword the sentence to show that Cornelius told the story to each of the following in turn. (Remember that you must check the declension of each noun before you can produce the correct ending.):

Septimus, Flāvia, puellae, mīles, puerī,
raedārius, senātōrēs, caupō, viātōrēs.

Exercise 21b

The sentence **Eucleidēs mandāta servīs dabat** can be translated
Eucleides was giving orders to the slaves.
or
Eucleides was giving the slaves orders.

Translate each of the following sentences in two ways:

1. Patruus pecūniam puerīs dat.
2. Māter fābulam puellae nārrāvit.
3. Ōrātōrēs fābulās cīvibus nārrāvērunt.
4. Ancilla invīta caupōnī cibum trādit.
5. Caupōnēs rārō cēnam senātōribus dant.   **rārō,** seldom
6. Omnia patrī meō semper dīcō.
7. Nihil lēgātō prīncipis dīxit.

Note

The dative case is also found with **licet** and **appropinquāre**, e.g.:

Mihi licet exīre.	*It is permissible for me to go out.*
	I am allowed to go out. I may go out.
Urbī appropinquābant.	*They were coming near to the city.*
	They were approaching the city.

Exercise 21c

Read aloud and translate:

1. Mātrēs līberōrum multa eīs dīcunt.
2. Dāvus Cornēliī mandāta servīs dedit.
3. Cornēliī mox urbis portīs appropinquābant.
4. Cornēlius epistulam ad Titum mīsit et omnia eī explicāvit.
5. Puerīs nōn licēbat sōlīs per viās errāre.
6. Marcus, "Tacē, Sexte!" inquit. "Nōbīs nōn licet hīc clāmāre."
7. Dum Cornēliī urbī appropinquābant, Titus omnia eīs parābat.

Building Up the Meaning IV
NOUNS: Dative or Ablative?

You will have noticed that the dative and ablative cases often have identical endings, e.g., **servō, puellīs, mīlitibus.** How are you to tell which case is used in a particular sentence? The Latin will usually provide clues to help you decide correctly:

a. Is the noun preceded by a preposition? If it is, the noun will be in the ablative case because no preposition governs the dative case.
b. If there is no preposition, does the noun refer to a *person*? If it does, it will normally be in the dative because nouns referring to persons are usually governed by a preposition if they are in the ablative. If the noun refers to a *thing*, it is more likely to be ablative than dative.

Consider the following sentences, noting the clues provided by each word and group of words as you meet them:

1. Canem nostrum puerō dedit.
The words **canem nostrum** are obviously accusative. When we reach **puerō,** knowing that **puer** refers to a person, we can say that it must be in the dative case because it would be governed by a preposition if it was in the ablative case. A Roman reading as far as **puerō** would have known before he reached the verb that someone was transferring "our dog" in some way or other "to the boy."

2. Puerō canem nostrum dedimus.
The fact that **puerō** comes first in the sentence does not alter the reasoning. Since it refers to a person and is not governed by a preposition, it must be in the dative case and, again, some transfer is taking place.

3. Canem nostrum baculō verberat.
When we come to **baculō,** knowing that **baculum** refers to a thing, we can be sure because of the sense that it is in the ablative case. A Roman would have understood as soon as he reached **baculō** that someone was "doing" something to our dog *with* a stick.

4. Baculō canem nostrum verberat.
Again, the fact that **baculō** appears as the first word makes no difference. We again know that **baculō** must be in the ablative case because it refers to a thing, and when we come to **canem** we know that someone is "doing" something to our dog *with* a stick.

Exercise 21d

Look carefully for the type of clue mentioned in the preceding discussion to help you with the words which could be dative or ablative. Identify each as dative or ablative and then translate the entire sentence.

1. Caupō viātōribus cibum dedit.
2. Servus mūrem baculō necāvit.
3. Raedārius equōs habēnīs dēvertēbat.
4. Amīcō captīvī aurum trādidī.
5. Puellae lupum virgīs repellunt.
6. Necesse erat pecūniam praedōnibus trādere.
7. Puerī pontem in rīvō rāmīs faciēbant.
8. Epistulās prīncipis tabellāriīs dedistī.
9. Aurīga habēnās manibus arripuit.
10. Senātor fīliīs fābulās narrat.
11. Servus nōmina virōrum dominō dīxit.
12. Bovēs clāmōribus incitāmus.
13. Vīlicus bovem ē rīvō manibus extrāxit.
14. Frāter meus captīvōs aurō adiūvit.
15. Mercātōrēs togās et tunicās cīvibus mōnstrant.

> captīvus, -ī (m), captive
> aurum, -ī (n), gold
> pecūnia, -ae (f), money
> praedō, praedōnis (m), robber
> pōns, pontis (m), bridge
> mercātor, mercātōris (m), merchant
> mōnstrō (1), to show

CAECILIAE
Q·CRETICI·F
METELLAE·CRASSI

I

Caeciliae
Q. Crēticī f(īliae)
Metellae Crassī

(the tomb) of Caecilia Metella, daughter of Q(uintus Caecilius Metellus)
Creticus, (wife) of Crassus

II

D. M. S. CRISPINAE CONIUGI DIVINAE, NUTRICI SENATORUM
DUUM, ALBUS CONIUNX, C. Q. F. AN. XVII, H. VIX. AN. XXX
M. II.B. M. F.

D(īs) m(ānibus) s(acrum) Crispīnae coniugī dīvīnae, nūtrīcī senātōrum
du(ōr)um, Albus coniunx, c(um) q(uō) f(ēlīciter) an(nōs) XVII (vīxit), h(oc
monumentum fēcit). Vīx(it) an(nōs) XXX m(ēnsēs) II. B(ene) m(erentī)
f(ēcit).

Sacred to the deified spirits of Crispina, divine wife, nurse of two senators;
Albus her husband, with whom she lived happily seventeen years, (set up
this monument). She lived thirty years, two months. He made (this for her)
who well deserved it.

III

D(īs) M(ānibus) Iūliae Velvae piētissimae. Vīxit an(nōs) L. Aurēl(ius) Mer-
curiālis hēr(ēs) faciundum cūrāvit. Vīvus sibi et suīs fēcit.

To the deified spirits of Julia Velva, a most dutiful woman. She lived 50
years. Aurelius Mercurialis, her heir, had this (tomb) made. He made it for
himself and his family while he was still alive.

Word Study VI

The Supine Stem

The stem of the supine (fourth principal part) of a Latin verb may be the source of other Latin words and English derivatives. This stem is found by dropping the -um from the supine, e.g., the supine stem of **vīsum** is **vīs-**. Here are some common types of words formed from the supine stem:

1. No suffix.
   The supine stem may form an English word with no change:
   invent (**inventum**)   fact (**factum**)

2. Silent -e.
   An English word may be formed by adding silent -e to the supine stem:
   narrate (**nārrātum**)   finite (**fīnītum**)

3. Suffix -or.
   When added to the supine stem, the Latin suffix -or creates a 3rd declension, masculine noun, which means "one who does" the action of the verb. These nouns are often borrowed into English with no change in spelling, although there is sometimes a change in meaning:

Supine	Latin Noun & Meaning	English Word
nārrātum (nārrāre)	**nārrātor, nārrātōris** (*m*), story-teller	narrator
spectātum (spectāre)	**spectātor, spectātōris** (*m*), onlooker, observer	spectator
āctum (agere)	**āctor, āctōris** (*m*), driver, doer, actor	actor

4. Suffix -iō.
   The Latin suffix -iō, when added to the supine stem, forms a 3rd declension, feminine noun, which means the "act of," "state of," or "result of" the action of the verb. The genitive singular of these nouns ends in -iōnis, and the base has -iōn-, which is the source of English words ending in -sion and -tion. The meaning of the English word is similar or identical to that of the Latin noun, which takes its meaning from the Latin verb:

Supine	Latin Noun & Meaning	English Word
vīsum (vidēre)	**vīsiō, vīsiōnis** (*f*), act of viewing	vision
nārrātum (nārrāre)	**nārrātiō, nārrātiōnis** (*f*), act of telling (a story)	narration

Note that whether the English word ends in -sion or -tion depends on whether the supine from which it is derived ends in -sum or -tum.

48

Exercise 1

Using the above information, give a 3rd declension Latin noun and an English derivative for each of the following supines. Check in a Latin dictionary to verify the existence of each noun and compare its meaning with that of its English derivative.

1. audītum (audīre)
2. cautum (cavēre)
3. exclāmātum (exclāmāre)
4. factum (facere)
5. mānsum (manēre)
6. missum (mittere)
7. petītum (petere)
8. positum (pōnere)
9. statum (stāre)

Exercise 2

Give the meaning of each English word below. Then give the supine, infinitive, and the meaning of the verb from which the English word is derived.

1. apparition
2. cogitate
3. diction
4. habitation
5. inventor
6. motor
7. session
8. state
9. tacit

Latin Expressions in English

Latin phrases and expressions are often used in English. Some are very familiar, such as **et cetera** (etc.), *and the rest*. Others are more specialized, such as **ipso facto**, *by the fact itself*, a legal expression used to describe an assumption that has obvious truth, e.g., "A slave, ipso facto, had no right to vote."

While Latin expressions may sometimes be used in English as mere affectations, there are occasions when they are very effective in summarizing an idea succinctly. For example, the term *de facto segregation* refers to a long history of racial segregation which occurred *in fact*, even though no legal measures were taken to achieve it. **De jure** segregation, on the other hand, was achieved *by law*. These two Latin phrases capsulize these notions in a minimum of words, thereby making communication more efficient.

Exercise 3

Look up the following Latin expressions in an English dictionary. Use each expression in a sentence which illustrates its special use in English.

1. ad hoc
2. ad infinitum
3. modus operandi
4. non sequitur
5. per capita
6. per se
7. quid pro quo
8. sine qua non
9. status quo

22
At the Porta Capena

Intereā Titus, patruus Marcī et Cornēliae, eōs prope Portam Capēnam exspectābat. Cīvēs, mercātōrēs, servī per portam ībant atque hūc illūc currēbant. Titus tamen in lectīcā sedēbat. Ubi Cornēliōs cōnspexit, ē lectīcā dēscendit. Ē raedā dēscendērunt Cornēliī. Interdiū enim raedās intrā urbem agere Rōmānīs nōn licēbat.   5

Stupuit Sextus ubi multitūdinem cīvium, servōrum turbam vīdit. Undique erat strepitus plaustrōrum, undique clāmor mercātōrum, viātōrum, raedāriōrum.

Titus Cornēlium et Aurēliam et līberōs maximō cum gaudiō salūtāvit. "Quam laetus," inquit, "vōs omnēs excipiō! Nōnne estis itinere dēfessī?"   10

"Valdē dēfessī," respondit Cornēlius. "Mihi necesse est celeriter ad Cūriam īre, sed prīmum Aurēliam et Cornēliam domum dūcam."

"Ita vērō!" inquit Titus. "Ecce! Lectīcāriī, quōs vōbīs condūxī, vōs domum ferent. Ego puerōs cūrābō. Multa et mīra vidēbunt puerī, atque ego omnia eīs explicābō."   15

Itaque per viās urbis lectīcāriī patrem, mātrem, fīliam celeriter domum tulērunt. Postquam eō advēnērunt, Aurēlia et Cornēlia, itinere dēfessae, sē quiētī dedērunt. Cornēlius tamen sē lāvit, togam pūram induit, iterum in lectīcā cōnsēdit.

"Ad Cūriam celeriter!" inquit.   20

hūc illūc, this way and that	**prīmum,** first
lectīca, -ae (*f*), litter	**domum,** homeward, home
interdiū, during the day	**dūcam,** I will take
stupeō (2), to be amazed, gape	**ferent,** (they) will carry
turba, -ae (*f*), crowd, mob	**cūrābō,** I will take care of
undique, on all sides	**multa et mīra,** many wonderful things
strepitus, noise, clattering	**vidēbunt,** (they) will see
maximō cum gaudiō, with very great joy	**eō,** there, to that place
Cūria, -ae (*f*), Senate House	**quiēs, quiētis** (*f*), rest
	pūrus, -a, -um, clean

currō, currere (3), cucurrī, cursum, to run
sedeō, sedēre (2), sēdī, sessum, to sit
dēscendō, dēscendere (3), dēscendī, dēscēnsum, to climb down
agō, agere (3), ēgī, āctum, to do, drive
condūcō, condūcere (3), condūxī, conductum, to hire
ferō, ferre, tulī, lātum, to carry, bring, bear
induō, induere (3), induī, indūtum, to put on
cōnsīdō, cōnsīdere (3), cōnsēdī, to sit down

Slaves carrying a lectīca.

Exercise 22a

Respondē Latīnē:

1. Quis Cornēliōs prope Portam Capēnam exspectābat?
2. Quī hūc illūc currēbant per portam?
3. Ubi sedēbat Titus?
4. Cūr Cornēliī ē raedā dēscendērunt?
5. Quid Sextus prope portam vīdit et audīvit?
6. Quōmodo Titus Cornēliōs salūtāvit?
7. Suntne Cornēliī itinere dēfessī?
8. Quō necesse est Cornēliō īre?
9. Quis lectīcāriōs condūxit?
10. Quis puerīs multa et mīra explicābit?
11. Quid fēcit Cornēlius postquam domum Cornēliī advēnērunt?

51

VERBS: Future Tense I

Look at these sentences:

Ego omnia eīs **explicābō**.	I will **explain** *everything to them.*
Multa et mīra **vidēbunt** puerī.	The boys will **see** *many wonderful things.*
Ego Cornēliam domum **dūcam**.	I will **take** *Cornelia home.*
Brevī tempore ad Portam Capēnam **adveniēmus**.	*In a short time* we will **arrive** *at the Porta Capena.*

The words in bold type are examples of the *future tense*. The endings of the future tense are shown in the table below:

			1st and 2nd Conjugations	3rd and 4th Conjugations
		1	*-bō*	*-am*
	Singular	2	*-bis*	*-ēs*
		3	*-bit*	*-et*
		1	*-bimus*	*-ēmus*
	Plural	2	*-bitis*	*-ētis*
		3	*-bunt*	*-ent*

Note that in the future tense the endings of verbs in the 3rd and 4th conjugations are quite different from the endings of verbs in the 1st and 2nd conjugations.

Note also that the **e** of the ending in the 3rd and 4th conjugations is short before final *-t* and *-nt.*

Learn the forms of the future tense, as follows:

		1st Conjugation	2nd Conjugation	3rd Conjugation		4th Conjugation
Infinitive		par*āre*	hab*ēre*	mitt*ere*	iac*ere* (*-iō*)	aud*īre*
Singular	1	parā*bō*	habē*bō*	mitt*am*	iaci*am*	audi*am*
	2	parā*bis*	habē*bis*	mitt*ēs*	iaci*ēs*	audi*ēs*
	3	parā*bit*	habē*bit*	mitt*et*	iaci*et*	audi*et*
Plural	1	parā*bimus*	habē*bimus*	mitt*ēmus*	iaci*ēmus*	audi*ēmus*
	2	parā*bitis*	habē*bitis*	mitt*ētis*	iaci*ētis*	audi*ētis*
	3	parā*bunt*	habē*bunt*	mitt*ent*	iaci*ent*	audi*ent*

Exercise 22b

Read aloud and translate:

1. Titus nōs prope Portam Capēnam exspectābit; omnēs maximō cum gaudiō salūtābit.
2. Hodiē sepulcra magna Rōmānōrum praeclārōrum vīdimus; crās Cūriam et alia aedificia Rōmāna vidēbimus.
3. Fortasse patruus noster nōs ad Cūriam dūcet.
4. Cornēliī omnēs sē parant; brevī tempore ad urbem iter facient.
5. Multa et mīra vident puerī; lectīcāriī eōs mox domum portābunt.
6. Cornēlius ē raedā dēscendet, nam raedam intrā urbem agere nōn licet.
7. Quam diū in urbe manēbis, pater?
8. Bene dormiētis, puerī. Longum enim iter hodiē fēcistis.
9. Cornēlia, itinere longō dēfessa, sē quiētī dabit.
10. Puerī multa rogābunt dē aedificiīs quae in urbis viīs vidēbunt.
11. Crās, ubi surgētis, puerī, strepitum plaustrōrum audiētis.
12. Titus, ubi puerōs domum dūcet, omnia eīs explicābit.

> **maneō, manēre** (2), **mānsī, mānsum,** to remain, stay
> **faciō, facere** (3), **fēcī, factum,** to make, do

Note that in sentences 11 and 12 the verbs in the clauses introduced by **ubi** are in the future tense. English, however, requires the present tense here.

Exercise 22c

Add one of the following adverbs to each sentence, according to the tense of the verb: **hodiē** *(present),* **heri** *(perfect), or* **crās** *(future). Read aloud and translate:*

1. Mīlitēs ad urbem _____ veniunt.
2. Puerōs parentēs ad cubiculum _____ mīsērunt.
3. Multī hominēs in viā _____ stābunt.
4. Lectīcāriī ad portam _____ venient.
5. Multae mātrēs līberōs _____ expectāvērunt.
6. Senātōrēs mīlitēs _____ cōnspiciunt.
7. Aedificia multa _____ vīdimus.
8. Cūr nōn caupōnem _____ petēmus?
9. Nōs omnēs in raedā _____ sedēmus.
10. Vōs in lectīs _____ dormiētis.

> **Quandō cadet Rōma, cadet et mundus.** *When Rome falls, the world will fall, too.* (Medieval pilgrims' proverb; Venerable Bede)

Exercise 22d

Take parts, read aloud, and translate:

Intereā Eucleidēs et puerī cum Titō extrā Portam Capēnam stābant.

TITUS: Salvēte, puerī! Quid in itinere vīdistis? Vīdistisne rūsticōs in agrīs? Agrōsne colēbant?

SEXTUS: Rūsticōs vīdimus. Agrōs nōn colēbant, sed sub arboribus quiēscēbant. At caupōnam vīdimus; nostra raeda in fossā haerēbat et nōbīs necesse 5 erat in caupōnā pernoctāre.

MARCUS: Ita vērō! Gaudēbam quod pater meus in illā caupōnā pernoctāre cōnstituit. Caupō erat vir Graecus, amīcus Eucleidis.

SEXTUS: Ego quoque gaudēbam, nam mīles bonam fābulam nōbīs narrāvit. In illā fābulā caupō quīdam hospitem necāvit. Tālēs fābulās amō. 10

MARCUS: Sed quid nunc faciēmus, patrue? Ego volō Cūriam et Forum vidēre.

SEXTUS: Quandō Circum Maximum vīsitābimus? Ecce! Nōnne Circum Maximum suprā mūrōs urbis exstantem vidēre possum?

MARCUS: Ita vērō! Est Circus Maximus. Nōn procul abest.

TITUS: Nōn possumus omnia hodiē vidēre. Crās satis temporis habēbimus. 15

SEXTUS: Sed quid est illud aedificium? Nōnne pontem ingentem suprā portam videō?

MARCUS: Nōn pontem hīc vidēs, ō stulte! Est aquaeductus, Aqua Marcia. Per illum aquaeductum Rōmānī aquam in urbem ferunt. Cavē imbrem, Sexte! 20

SEXTUS: Sed nōn pluit.

TITUS: Semper hīc pluit, Sexte. Rīmōsa enim est Aqua Marcia.

extrā (+ *acc.*), outside
at, but
tālis, -is, -e, such
Circus Maximus, a stadium in Rome
  maximus, -a, -um, very great, greatest, very large
suprā (+ *acc.*), above
mūrus, -ī (*m*), wall

exstantem, standing out, towering
satis temporis, enough time
stultus, -a, -um, stupid
aqua, -ae (*f*), water
Cavē imbrem! Watch out for the rain!
rīmōsus, -a, -um, full of cracks, leaky

colō, colere (3), coluī, cultum, to cultivate
quiēscō, quiēscere (3), quiēvī, quiētum, to rest, keep quiet
cōnstituō, cōnstituere (3), cōnstituī, cōnstitūtum, to decide
pluit, pluere (3), pluit, it rains (usually found only in 3rd person singular and infinitive)

Exercise 22e

Give the appropriate form of the future tense for each verb in parentheses:

1. Nōs in Viā Appiā nōn (pernoctāre).
2. Mox vōs urbī (appropinquāre) et patruum (cōnspicere).
3. Titus multās fābulās dē aedificiīs Rōmae puerīs (nārrāre).
4. Ego prīmum Aurēliam et Cornēliam domum (dūcere).
5. Puerī multa et mīra in urbe crās (vidēre).
6. Quandō Cornēlius ad Cūriam (venīre)?
7. Tū cēnam bonam in illā caupōnā (habēre).
8. Nōs in lectīs sordidīs nōn (dormīre).
9. Crās Marcus et Sextus māne (surgere).
10. Cornēlius Titum frātrem (petere); mox eum (invenīre).

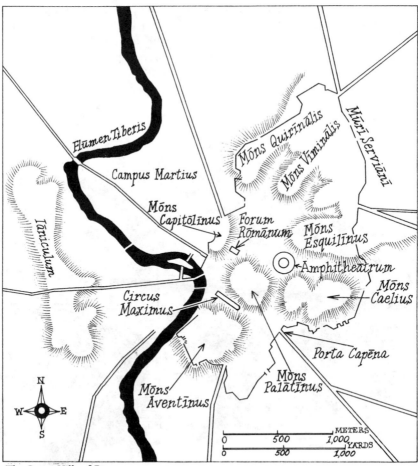

The Seven Hills of Rome

Aqueducts

One feature of the city which the Cornelii would notice as they approached Rome was the evidence of the Romans' passion for water. Abundant water for baths and fountains and lakes was an utter necessity to the Roman, so that it had to be brought in by the aqueducts whose arches strode into Rome from all directions. By A.D. 80, nine aqueducts were in use, carrying water across the plain to Rome from sources up to fifty-six miles or ninety kilometers distant.

The illustration shows the arches supporting the water-channel and a cross-section of the channel itself. To maintain the downhill flow, experts recommended a fall of six inches or fifteen centimeters in every ninety-eight feet or thirty meters. Tunnels, with inspection shafts built into them, were driven through hills which it was impossible to by-pass. Sometimes, by using the principle that water rises to its own level, a U-shaped arrangement of the tunnel allowed an uphill flow. Responsibility for maintaining and cleaning the whole vast system rested with the **cūrātor aquārum** and his staff.

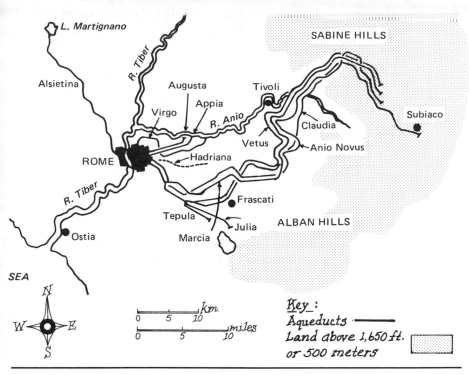

Routes of the Roman aqueducts.

The first aqueduct, the **Aqua Appia,** went underground. Since a gravity system was employed, later ones had to be higher to serve the hillier districts of the town. The Romans then hit on the idea of using arches to support the water-channel. The arches turned out to be beautiful structures in themselves, but the Romans had adopted them for quite different reasons. They stood up better to earthquakes, always a hazard in Italy; the wind could blow through them, where a solid wall would invite disaster; and they could be easily repaired, as workmen could take the building materials from one side to the other.

Admiring comments about the aqueducts abound from native and foreigner alike. "Just as impressive," says one writer, "as the pyramids, but how much more useful!" Not only so, but we also have an astonishing book, *De aquis urbis Romae,* by Frontinus, Superintendent of Aqueducts, written about A.D. 97, describing the system in detail and the difficulties of organizing and maintaining it. He reports that, through bribery of watermen, supplies were sometimes diverted into private estates and never reached Rome at all. Householders in Rome itself often succeeded in bribing inspectors (who were, after all, slaves) to replace a narrow pipe by one of wider bore, while they continued to pay at the old rate!

According to the latest available figures, the daily consumption of water in a large city today is about 120 gallons or 455 liters per person. According to Frontinus, in his day the Roman aqueducts could deliver over 264 million gallons or one billion liters in twenty-four hours, providing a daily allowance of about 240 gallons or 900 liters per person! The aqueducts leaked dreadfully, as the Cornelii found at the Porta Capena, and what with water thieves and corrupt inspectors, all this water did not actually reach Rome. For all that, the Roman citizen still had a lot of water at his disposal. Did he use it all? The answer is "Yes," because as one Roman writer put it, "The waters, having provided the city with the life-giving element, passed on into the sewers." The Roman, you see, hardly ever turned the tap off. For him, running water was simply running water!

A Roman Contemplates the Aqueducts

We must now describe marvels which are unsurpassed for their genuine value. Quintus Marcius Rex (praetor 144–143 B.C.), having been ordered by the senate to repair the channels of the **Aqua Appia** (the earliest aqueduct, built by Appius Claudius Caecus in 312 B.C.), the **Aniō Vetus** (begun in 272 B.C.), and the **Tepula,** drove underground passages through the mountains and brought to Rome a new water-supply named after himself (the **Aqua Marcia**) and completed within the period of his praetorship.

Agrippa, moreover, as aedile added to these the **Aqua Virgō** (completed in 19 B.C.), repaired the channels of the others and put them in order, and constructed 700 basins, not to speak of 500 fountains and 130 reservoirs for distribution of water, many of the latter being richly decorated. On these works he erected 300 bronze or marble statues and 400 marble pillars marking the course taken by the channels. All of this he did in a year. In the memoirs of his aedileship he adds that in celebration of these achievements games lasting 59 days were held and that the bathing establishments were opened to the public free of charge—all 170 of them, a number which at Rome has now been infinitely increased.

All of these previous aqueducts have been surpassed by the most recent and very costly work inaugurated by the Emperor Gaius (A.D. 37–41) and completed by Claudius (A.D. 41–54), who made the Curtian and Caerulean Springs and the **Aniō Novus** flow into Rome from the 40th milestone at such a high level as to supply water to all the seven hills of the city. 350,000,000 sesterces were spent on this work.

If we carefully consider the abundant supplies of water in public buildings, baths, pools, open channels, private houses, gardens, and country estates near the city; if we consider the distances traversed by the water before it arrives, the raising of arches, the tunneling of mountains, and the building of level routes across deep valleys, we shall readily admit that there has never been anything more remarkable in the whole world.

Pliny, *Natural History* XXXVI. 121–123

VERBS: *Future Tense II*

The following are the future tenses of the irregular verbs you have met:

Infinitive			esse	posse	velle	nōlle	īre	ferre
Number and Person	*Singular*	1	erō	poterō	volam	nōlam	ībō	feram
		2	eris	poteris	volēs	nōlēs	ībis	ferēs
		3	erit	poterit	volet	nōlet	ībit	feret
	Plural	1	erimus	poterimus	volēmus	nōlēmus	ībimus	ferēmus
		2	eritis	poteritis	volētis	nōlētis	ībitis	ferētis
		3	erunt	poterunt	volent	nōlent	ībunt	ferent

Note that velle, nōlle, īre, and ferre have future tense endings like those of regular verbs. Note also where long vowels occur in the endings of these verbs.

Exercise 22f

Read aloud and translate:

1. Ībisne ad Cūriam, pater? Ita vērō! Ad Cūriam celeriter ībō.
2. Quandō domum redībis, pater? Nesciō.
3. Fortasse Cornēlius domum redīre brevī tempore poterit.
4. Eucleidēs ad amphitheātrum īre nōlet.
5. Necesse erit diū in urbe manēre.
6. Nocte vehicula magna onera in urbe ferent.
7. Puerī Circum Maximum crās vidēre volent.
8. Ubi līberī māne erunt? Tū līberōs nōn vidēbis, nam domō mox exībunt.
9. Sī equī strēnuē labōrābunt, raedam ē fossā extrahere poterunt.
10. Sī pluet, ad silvam ambulāre nōlam.
11. Ferēsne cistam meam in caupōnam? Minimē! Tū ipse eam fer!
12. Redībitisne ad vīllam rūsticam? Fortasse redīre poterimus.
13. Volētisne crās ad Circum Maximum īre? Ita vērō! Crās illūc īre volēmus.
14. "Ego īre nōlam," inquit Aurēlia.
15. Post cēnam puerī cubitum īre nōlent.

> **domō**, out of the house
> **exeō, exīre** (*irreg.*), **exiī, exitum**, to go out

Note that in sentences 9 and 10 the verbs in the clauses introduced by sī are in the future tense. English, however, requires the present tense here.

59

23
Always Tomorrow

Simulac Titus et puerī et Eucleidēs urbem per Portam Capēnam intrāvērunt, clāmāvit Sextus, "Quid nōs prīmum faciēmus? Quō ībimus? Vīsitābimusne — ?"

"Quō tū nōs dūcēs, patrue?" interpellāvit Marcus. "Vidēbimusne Cūriam et Forum?" 5

Titus, "Tacēte! Tacēte!" inquit. "Forum crās vīsitābimus. Crās, Eucleidēs, tibi licēbit puerōs eō dūcere. Tum erit satis temporis. Hodiē tamen, puerī, vōs domum per urbem dūcam et omnia in itinere vōbīs dēmōnstrābō."

Iam advēnerant ad Circum Maximum, quī nōn procul aberat. Stupuit Sextus ubi mōlem Circī Maximī vīdit. Stupuit quoque Marcus, quamquam 10 Circum anteā vīderat. Stupuit Titus, attonitus nōn mōle, sed silentiō Circī.

"Ēheu! Ēheu!" inquit Titus. "Hodiē Circus est clausus. Tribus diēbus tamen prīnceps ipse lūdōs magnificōs faciet."

"Nōnne tū nōs eō dūcēs?" rogāvit Marcus.

"Ēheu! Ego nōn poterō vōs dūcere," inquit Titus. "Fortasse Eucleidēs 15 vōs dūcet."

"Minimē!" respondit Sextus. "Librōs, nōn lūdōs amat Eucleidēs."

"Agite, puerī!" interpellāvit Titus. "Nunc circumībimus Montem Palātīnum et Forum intrābimus ad arcum Tiberiī. Ibi fortasse patrī tuō occurrēmus, Marce. Mox senātōrēs ē Cūriā exībunt." 20

Itaque Circum relīquērunt et Palātīnum circumiērunt. Titus in itinere mōnstrāvit puerīs mīra aedificia quae prīncipēs in Palātīnō aedificāverant. Tandem ad arcum Tiberiī advēnērunt, iam labōre et aestū dēfessī.

"Hic est arcus," inquit Titus, "quem — "

"Omnia vidēre poteritis crās," interpellāvit Cornēlius, quī eō ipsō tempore 25 ad arcum ē Cūriā advēnerat. "Eucleidēs omnia vōbīs explicābit. Iam sērō est. Agite! Iam domum ībimus."

---

simulac, as soon as
advēnerant, they had arrived
mōlēs, mōlis (*f*), mass, huge bulk
vīderat, he had seen
attonitus, -a, -um, astonished, astounded
clausus, -a, -um, closed
lūdī, -ōrum (*m pl*), games

liber, librī (*m*), book
Mōns Palātīnus, Montis Palātīnī (*m*), the Palatine Hill
arcus, arch
aedificō (1), to build
aestū, by the heat
quem (*acc.*), which

licet, licēre (2), licuit, it is allowed (usually found only in 3rd person singular and infinitive)

possum, posse (*irreg.*), potuī, to be able

circumeō, circumīre, circumiī, circumitum, to go around

occurrō, occurrere (3), occurrī, occursum (+ *dat.*), to meet, encounter

relinquō, relinquere (3), relīquī, relictum, to leave

Tantae mōlis erat Rōmānam condere gentem! *It was such a vast undertaking to found the Roman nation!* (Vergil, *Aeneid* I.33)

Cūriam et continēns eī Chalcidicum . . . fēcī. *I built the Curia and the Chalcidicum next to it.* (Augustus, *Res gestae* XIX)

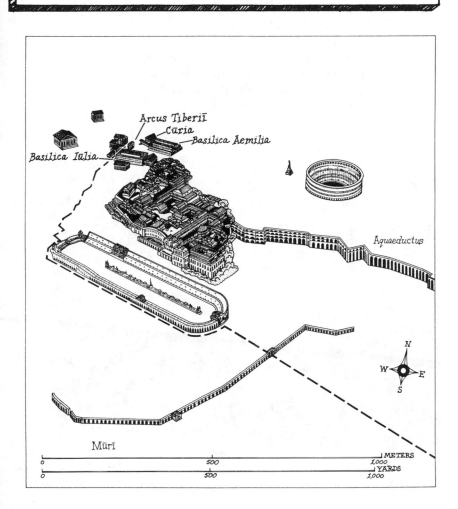

Exercise 23a

Respondē Latīnē:

1. Quid facere volēbant Sextus et Marcus postquam urbem intrāvērunt?
2. Quis puerōs crās ad Forum dūcet?
3. Quid Titus hodiē facere vult?
4. Vīderatne Sextus anteā Circum Maximum?
5. Stupuitne Marcus ubi Circum Maximum vīdit?
6. Eratne Titus attonitus mōle Circī?
7. Cūr Circum hodiē puerī nōn intrant?
8. Quid faciet prīnceps tribus diēbus?
9. Dūcetne Titus puerōs ad lūdōs?
10. Quid amat Eucleidēs?
11. Ubi occurrent puerī Cornēliō?
12. Quī mīra aedificia in Palātīnō aedificāverant?
13. Dēfessīne puerī ad arcum Tiberiī advēnērunt?
14. Quis puerīs prope arcum Tiberiī occurrit?
15. Quō Cornēlius puerōs hodiē dūcet?

Roman Magistrates and Lictors; an oil painting by Jean Lemaire (1598–1659). Montreal Museum of Fine Arts.

VERBS: *Pluperfect Tense*

Look at these sentences:

Iam **advēnerant** ad Circum.	*They had already reached the Circus.*
Circum anteā **vīderat.**	*He had seen the Circus before.*
Mīra aedificia **aedificāverant.**	*They had built marvelous buildings.*

The verbs in these sentences are all in the *pluperfect tense*, which can nearly always be translated into English by the word "had."

The endings of the pluperfect tense are the same for *all* Latin verbs:

	1 *-eram*		1 *-erāmus*
Singular	2 *-erās*	Plural	2 *-erātis*
	3 *-erat*		3 *-erant*

These endings are added to the perfect stem, which is found by dropping the ī from the end of the third principal part, e.g., **relīquī**, stem **relīqu-**.

	1 relīqu*eram*		1 relīqu*erāmus*
Singular	2 relīqu*erās*	Plural	2 relīqu*erātis*
	3 relīqu*erat*		3 relīqu*erant*

Exercise 23b

Read aloud and translate:

1. Eucleidēs puerōs ad urbem dūxerat et omnia eīs dēmōnstrāverat.
2. Aurēlia sollicita erat quod servī cēnam nōndum parāverant.
3. Hodiē librum diū legēbam quem mihi herī dedistī.
4. Dēfessus eram quod multās epistulās iam scrīpseram.
5. Vix domum advēnerātis, puerī, cum Eucleidēs in hortum intrāvit.

> **scrībo, scrībere** (3), **scrīpsī, scrīptum,** to write
> **vix,** scarcely

Exercise 23c

Substitute the corresponding pluperfect form for each verb in parentheses, read the sentence aloud, and translate:

1. Tantum sonitum numquam anteā (audīmus) _____.
2. Marcus laetus fuit quod patrī prope Cūriam (occurrit) _____.
3. Via erat plēna hominum quī ad urbem (veniunt) _____.
4. Lectīcāriī, quī Cornēlium per urbis viās (ferunt) _____, extrā Cūriam eum exspectābant.
5. Titus, quod Circum (invēnit) _____ clausum, puerōs domum dūcēbat.

> **tantus, -a, -um,** so great, such a big
> **sonitus,** sound

Building Up the Meaning V
VERBS: Present or Future?

Look at these sentences:

Cornēlius multōs servōs habet.	*Cornelius has many slaves.*
Scelestōs servōs ad vīllam mittet.	*He will send the wicked slaves to the farm.*
Hodiē in caupōnā manēmus.	*Today we remain in the inn.*
Crās Rōmam adveniēmus.	*Tomorrow we will reach Rome.*

The endings -ēs, -et, -ēmus, -ētis, -ent can denote the present tense of verbs of the 2nd conjugation or the future tense of verbs of the 3rd and 4th conjugations. If there is an *i* before the *e*, the verb will be the future tense of a 3rd conjugation -iō verb or the future tense of a 4th conjugation verb.

Exercise 23d

Following the examples, identify the remainder of the verb forms below:

Verb	Conjugation	Tense	Meaning
habent	2	present	they have
mittent	3	future	they will send
vident			
iubent			
ascendent			
admovent			
dormient			
timent			
dūcent			
rīdent			
facient			

Exercise 23e

Look carefully at the verbs in the following sentences. Decide the conjugation number first (this will help you to get the tense right) and then read aloud and translate:

1. Puerī Eucleidem nōn vident, sed vōcem eius audient.
2. Vidēsne senātōrēs in viīs? Quandō Cornēlius veniet?
3. Servī celeriter current, nam Cornēlium timent.
4. Sextus māne surget; in animō habet exīre.
5. Ego et Cornēlia tacēmus; patrem timēmus.

Versiculī: *"Procrustes," pages 100–102.*

Review V

Exercise Va

Supply Latin words to match the English cues. Be sure to give the right endings. Read each sentence aloud and translate it.

1. Sextus fābulam dē caupōne _____ _____ nārrābat. (wicked) (to Cornelius)
2. Eucleidēs mandāta _____ et _____ dabat. (to the slaves) (to the slave-women)
3. Cūnctī Cornēliī ē _____ vēnērunt. (the inn)
4. Viātōrēs nōn in _____ caupōnīs bene cēnāre possunt. (all)
5. Raedārius habēnīs _____ verberāvit. (the horses)
6. Sextus _____ dē _____ _____ _____ nārrāvit. (everything) (the dead mouse) (to Marcus)
7. Dum Cornēlius fābulam _____ nārrat, _____ appropinquāvērunt. (to his wife) (the city)
8. Prope viam sunt sepulcra _____ _____ _____ _____. (of many famous Romans)
9. Titus _____ prope Portam Capēnam exspectābat. (them)
10. Interdiū raedās intrā urbem agere _____ nōn licēbat. (to or for them)
11. "Quam laetus _____ _____ videō!" exclāmat Titus. (all of you = you all)
12. "_____ sumus valdē dēfessī," respondet Cornēlius. (We)
13. "_____ necesse est ad Cūriam īre." (For me)
14. Titus respondet, "_____ lectīcāriōs condūxī." (For you)
15. "Ego multa et mīra _____ et _____ explicābō," inquit Titus. (to you) (to Sextus)
16. Postquam domum advēnit, Cornēlius _____ lāvit. (himself)
17. "_____ in caupōnā pernoctāre necesse erat," inquit Sextus. (For us)
18. Sextus _____ _____ suprā portam videt. (a huge aqueduct)
19. Crās Forum vīsitāre _____ licēbit. (to or for the boys)
20. Hodiē _____ dormīre licet. (to or for Cornelia)
21. _____ diēbus prīnceps lūdōs _____ faciet. (In three) (for the Romans)
22. _____ _____ Titus Marcum et Sextum dūcet. (To them, i.e., the games)
23. Cornēlius ē Cūriā mox exībit. _____ Marcus et Sextus occurrent. (Him)
24. Titus mīra aedificia _____ mōnstrāvit. (to the boys)
25. Crās multa alia aedificia _____ mōnstrābit. (to them)

Exercise Vb

Give the requested forms of the following verbs in the present, imperfect, future, perfect, and pluperfect tenses:

	Present	Imperfect	Future	Perfect	Pluperfect
1. circumīre (3rd pl.)	_____	_____	_____	_____	_____
2. dēscendere (2nd sing.)	_____	_____	_____	_____	_____
3. ferre (2nd pl.)	_____	_____	_____	_____	_____
4. dare (1st pl.)	_____	_____	_____	_____	_____
5. esse (3rd sing.)	_____	_____	_____	_____	_____
6. respondēre (1st sing.)	_____	_____	_____	_____	_____
7. surgere (3rd pl.)	_____	_____	_____	_____	_____
8. cōgitāre (2nd sing.)	_____	_____	_____	_____	_____
9. conicere (1st sing.)	_____	_____	_____	_____	_____
10. venīre (1st pl.)	_____	_____	_____	_____	_____

Exercise Vc

Read the following passage and answer the questions below with full sentences in Latin:

Cornēlius, postquam in triclīnium intrāvit, Cornēliam vīdit. Cornēlia pictūram, quae in mūrō erat, spectābat.

"Quid tū facis, mea fīlia?" inquit Cornēlius.

Cui Cornēlia, "Hanc pictūram valdē amō, pater. Nōnne hic vir est Herculēs? Eucleidēs nōbīs multa dē Hercule dīxit, sed ego omnia audīre volō." 5

Respondit Cornēlius, "Herculēs, ut bene scīs, erat vir Graecus. Ōlim, ubi īnfāns erat et in lectō dormiēbat, subitō duo serpentēs lectō appropinquāvērunt et Herculem dormientem necāre volēbant. Sed Herculēs, ē somnō excitātus, serpentēs sōlus strangulāvit."

Cornēlia tamen rogāvit, "Sed cūr in pictūrā est canis triformis? Cūr Herculēs 10 hunc canem trahit?"

Eī respondit Cornēlius, "Herculēs, quod dēmēns fīliōs suōs ōlim necāverat, miser erat et sē pūnīre cōnstituit. Itaque factus est servus dominī cuiusdam scelestī quī eum valdē timēbat et multōs labōrēs perficere iussit. Ille canis, quem in pictūrā vidēs, est Cerberus quī portās Īnferōrum custōdit. In hāc 15 pictūrā Herculēs ex Īnferīs dūcit Cerberum invītum. Dominus enim Herculis eum in Īnferōs dēscendere iusserat, quod ita cōgitābat: 'Herculēs numquam ex Īnferīs redībit. Cerberus certē eum necābit.' Sed tandem exiit ex Īnferīs Herculēs cum cane, nam omnia perficere solēbat. Itaque dominus perterritus Herculem canem ad Īnferōs statim redūcere iussit." 20

At iam Cornēlia et pater vōcem Aurēliae audīvērunt. "Ēheu!" clāmāvit Cornēlia. "Māter nōs vocat. Mox erit cēnae tempus."

"Ita vērō!" respondit Cornēlius. "Senātōrēs quīdam apud nōs cēnābunt. Necesse est mihi mātrem tuam cōnsulere. Crās tamen dē aliīs Herculis labōribus tibi nārrābō." 25

triclīnium, -ī (n), dining room
ut bene scīs, as you know well
excitātus, -a, -um, wakened, aroused
triformis, -is, -e, three-headed
dēmēns, in a fit of madness

factus est, became
cuiusdam, genitive of quīdam
Īnferī, -ōrum, (m pl), the underworld
apud nōs, at our home

perficiō, perficere (3), perfēcī, perfectus, to accomplish

1. What does Cornelia love?
2. What does Cornelia want to hear?
3. What did the snakes do?
4. What is Hercules doing with the dog in the picture?
5. Why did Hercules decide to punish himself?
6. Who is Cerberus?
7. Why did the master order Hercules to descend into the underworld?
8. What did the master do when Hercules brought Cerberus to him?
9. Why does Cornelius have to consult with Aurelia?
10. When will Cornelia hear about other labors of Hercules?

Exercise Vd

1. *In the passage above, locate in sequence all of the verbs in the imperfect, perfect, pluperfect, and future tenses and translate them.*
2. *Locate all of the words in the dative case and translate the sentences in which they occur.*

67

24
First Morning in Rome

Iam diēs erat. Magnus erat clāmor in urbe. Iam canēs in viīs lātrābant, iam hominēs clāmābant et per viās currēbant. Servī ad Forum magnō tumultū onera ferēbant. Undique clāmor et strepitus! Sed nihil clāmōris, nihil strepitūs ad Marcum pervēnit. Neque clāmōrēs hominum neque lā-trātūs canum eum excitāverant. In lectō stertēbat nam dēfessus erat. 5

Sextus quoque in lectō manēbat sed dormīre nōn poterat. Numquam anteā urbem tantam vīsitāverat. Clāmōribus et strepitū excitātus, iam cōgi-tābat dē omnibus rēbus quās Titus heri narrāverat. "Quid hodiē vidēbimus? Fortasse cum Titō ībimus quī omnia nōbīs dēmōnstrābit. Cornēliusne nōs in Forum dūcet? Ego certē Forum et Cūriam et senātōrēs vidēre volō." 10

Intereā Eucleidēs, quī prīmā lūce exierat, iam domum redierat. Statim cubiculum puerōrum petīvit et, "Eho, puerī!" inquit. "Cūr nōndum sur-rēxistis? Abhinc duās hōrās ego surrēxī. Quod novum librum emere volēbam, in Argīlētum māne dēscendī ad tabernam quandam ubi in postibus nōmina multōrum poētārum vidēre potes. Catullus, Flaccus—" 15

At puerī celeriter interpellāvērunt quod Eucleidēs, ut bene sciēbant, semper aliquid novī docēre volēbat. "Quid in viā vīdistī?"

Eucleidēs, "Nihil," inquit, "nisi miserum hominem lapidibus oppres-sum. Bovēs lapidēs quadrātōs in plaustrō trahēbant ad novum aedificium quod Caesar prope Domum Auream aedificat. Illud aedificium est ingēns 20 amphitheātrum et mox—"

At puerī in cubiculō nōn iam manēbant, nam Eucleidēs, quī erat semper verbōsus, multa dē aedificiīs urbis narrāre solēbat; neque tamen puerī eum audīre volēbant.

---

magnō tumultū, with a great uproar
excitātus, -a, -um, aroused
dē omnibus rēbus, about all the things, about everything
Eho! Hey!
abhinc duās hōrās, two hours ago
novus, -a, -um, new
taberna, -ae (*f*), shop
ad tabernam quandam, to a certain shop
postis, postis (*m*), door-post

poēta, -ae (*m*), poet
ut, as
sciō (4), to know
aliquid, something
lapis, lapidis (*m*), stone
　　lapidibus oppressum, crushed by stones
　　lapidēs quadrātī, squared stones
quod, which
Domus Aurea, (Nero's) Golden House
neque tamen, but . . . not

perveniō, pervenīre (1), pervēnī, perventum, to arrive (at), reach
stertō, stertere (3), stertuī, to snore
redeō, redīre (*irreg.*), rediī, reditum, to return, go back
emō, emere (3), ēmī, ēmptum, to buy
doceō, docēre (2), docuī, doctum, to teach
trahō, trahere, (3), trāxī, tractum, to drag, pull

NOUNS: 4th and 5th Declensions

Most Latin nouns belong to the 1st, 2nd, or 3rd declensions. There are two other declensions to which a few nouns belong:

Number Case	4th Declension	5th Declension
Singular		
Nominative	man**us**	di**ēs**
Genitive	man**ūs**	di**ēī**
Dative	man**uī**	di**ēī**
Accusative	man**um**	di**em**
Ablative	man**ū**	di**ē**
Plural		
Nominative	man**ūs**	di**ēs**
Genitive	man**uum**	di**ērum**
Dative	man**ibus**	di**ēbus**
Accusative	man**ūs**	di**ēs**
Ablative	man**ibus**	di**ēbus**

Be sure to learn these forms thoroughly.

Nouns of the 4th and 5th declensions will appear in vocabularies as follows:

4th Declension

aestus, -ūs (*m*), heat
aquaeductus, -ūs (*m*), aqueduct
arcus, -ūs (*m*), arch
domus, -ūs (*f*), house
lātrātus, -ūs (*m*), barking
manus, -ūs (*f*), hand
rīsus, -ūs (*m*), smile, laugh
sonitus, -ūs (*m*), sound
strepitus, -ūs (*m*), noise, clattering
tumultus, -ūs (*m*), uproar, commotion

5th Declension

diēs, -ēī (*m*), day
rēs, reī (*f*), thing, matter, situation

Most 4th declension nouns are masculine; most 5th declension nouns are feminine.

Latin Phrases Used in English

ante meridiem, *before noon*
post meridiem, *after noon*
per diem, *a daily allowance for expenses*
in medias res, *into the middle of things*
in situ, *in its original place*

Exercise 24a

Read aloud and translate:

1. Mediā nocte tumultum magnum audīvī. Quae erat causa huius tumultūs? Magnō cum strepitū bovēs plaustra per viās trahēbant. Prīmum strepitus procul aberat; deinde in viā nostrā erat tumultus.

   huius, of this
   ·absum, abesse (*irreg.*), **āfuī,** to be away, absent, be distant

2. Multās rēs manibus nostrīs facimus. Eucleidēs manū stilum tenēbat, nam puerōs scrībere docēbat. Puerī arborēs manibus et pedibus anteā ascenderant. Manūs igitur eōrum sordidae erant. Eucleidēs eōs iussit manūs statim lavāre.

   stilus, -ī (*m*), pen   **eōrum,** their

3. Abhinc multōs diēs illa domus incēnsa est. Itaque dominus, quod mūrī domūs īnfirmī erant, domum novam ibi aedificāre cōnstituit. Ille dominus est senātor quī multās domūs in urbe habet. Omnēs eius domūs sunt magnae, sed domus nova erit omnium maxima. In hāc domō senātor ipse habitābit.

   incēnsa est, was burned

4. Multōs diēs in vīllā manēbāmus. Vēnit tamen diēs reditūs. Necesse erat iter septem diērum facere quod ad urbem celerrimē redīre volēbāmus. Eō diē discessimus. Sex diēs per Viam Appiam iter faciēbāmus. Septimō diē Rōmam pervēnimus.

   reditus, -ūs (*m*), return   **eō diē,** on that day
   discēdō, discēdere, (3), **discessī, discessum,** to go away, depart

5. Titus rem mīram nōbīs nārrāvit. Servus, quī nocte per viās urbis ambulābat, subitō fūgit perterritus. Quae erat causa huius reī? In viā occurrerat canī quī, ut ipse dīxit, tria capita habēbat. Dē tālibus rēbus in librīs saepe legimus sed numquam tālem rem ipsī vīdimus. Dē hāc rē omnēs cīvēs multās fābulās nārrant.

   caput, capitis (*n*), head
   fugiō, fugere (3), **fūgī, fugitum,** to flee
   legō, legere (3), **lēgī, lēctum,** to read

Selections from Catullus and Horace

I

Vīvāmus, mea Lesbia, atque amēmus,
rūmōrēsque senum sevēriōrum
omnēs ūnius aestimēmus assis!
Sōlēs occidere et redīre possunt;
nōbīs cum semel occidit brevis lūx,
nox est perpetua ūna dormienda.

Let us live, my Lesbia, and let us love,
and let us value all the gossips of the stern old men
as worth but a penny.
The sun is able to set and rise again;
for us when once our brief light has set,
one eternal night must be slept.
                              (Catullus, V. 1–6)

II

Tū nē quaesieris—scīre nefās—quem mihi, quem tibi
fīnem dī dederint, Leuconoē, . . . Dum loquimur, fūgerit invida
aetās: carpe diem, quam minimum crēdula posterō.

Don't inquire—it's wrong to know—what length of life the gods
have granted to you and to me, Leuconoe, . . . While we are talking, envious
time has fled; seize the day, putting as little trust as possible in the future.
                              (Horace, Odes I. 11–2 and 7–8)

III

Sunt quōs curriculō pulverem Olympicum
collēgisse iuvat mētaque fervidīs
ēvītāta rotīs palmaque nōbilis
terrārum dominōs ēvehit ad deōs.

Some people take pleasure in gathering
Olympic dust on the racetrack. When they narrowly
avoid the turning posts with their hot wheels, the noble
palm of victory exalts them as masters of the earth to the level of the gods.
                              (Horace, Odes I. 1. 3–6)

Rome

Impressions of Rome

What nation is so far distant, Caesar, or so barbarous that it does not have a representative at the games here in your city? Here come farmers from the Balkans, natives of South Russia nurtured on horse's blood, people from the banks of the Nile, as well as those from the Atlantic's farthest shores. Here too are Arabs, men from Southern Turkey, German tribesmen, and Ethiopians—all so different in dress and in appearance. Their speech too sounds all different; yet it is all one when you are hailed, Caesar, as the true father of our country.

Martial, De spectaculis III

Caecilius, in your own eyes you are a polished gentleman, but take my word for it, you are not. What are you then? A clown! You are like the hawker from across the Tiber who trades pale brimstone matches for broken glass or the man who sells to the idle bystanders soggy pease-pudding; like the keeper and trainer of snakes or the cheap slaves of the salt-sellers; like the hoarse-voiced seller of smoking sausages with his hot trays or a third-class street poet.

Martial, Epigrams I.41

If duty calls, the crowd gives way and the rich man is borne along rapidly over their heads by stout Liburnian bearers. On the way he will read, write, or sleep, for with the windows shut the litter induces sleep. Even so, he will get there before us. Though we hurry, the sea of humanity in front hinders us, and the great throng following jostles our backs. One man strikes us with his elbow, another with a hard pole; one knocks a beam against our heads, another a barrel. Our legs are plastered with mud, we are trampled on all sides by great feet, a soldier's hob-nailed boot crushes my toe. Newly patched togas are torn. A tall fir tree sways as the wagon rumbles on. Other carts carry pine trees, a nodding menace over the heads of the crowd. If the cart carrying Ligurian stone tilts forward and pours its overturned pile on the crowds, what remains of their bodies?

Juvenal, Satires III.239

The Streets of Rome

Roman houses were neither named nor numbered. Hence the very complicated instructions given to those wishing to reach a certain "address":

> Every time you meet me, Lupercus, you ask, "May I send a slave to fetch your book of poems? I'll return it as soon as I've read it." Lupercus, it's not worth troubling your slave. It's a long journey to the Pear Tree, and I live up three flights of steep stairs. You can find what you want closer to home. No doubt you often go down to the Argiletum. There's a shop opposite Caesar's Forum with both door-posts covered with advertisements so that you can in a moment read the names of all the poets. Look for me there.
>
> Martial, *Epigrams* I.117

SYRUS: I don't know the man's name, but I know where he lives.

DEMEA: Then tell me where.

SYRUS: Down here. You know the colonnade by the butcher's?

DEMEA: Of course I do.

SYRUS: Go straight up the street that way; a bit along there's a slope facing you; down there and after that, on this side here, there's a shrine with an alley beside it.

DEMEA: Where?

SYRUS: Near where the big wild fig-tree grows.

DEMEA: I've got it.

SYRUS: Down there.

DEMEA: But that's a dead end!

SYRUS: Ugh! What an idiot I am! I've made a mistake. Come right back to the colonnade again. Here's a much quicker and more direct route. Do you know the house of rich Cratinus?

DEMEA: Yes.

SYRUS: Go past it, down a street to the left; turn right at Diana's temple. Before you reach the gate, near the pool, there's a bakery with a carpenter's opposite. He's there.

> Terence, *Adelphi* 571

Domitian, who followed Titus as Emperor of Rome, issued an edict forbidding shopkeepers to display their wares on the streets. This, according to Martial, was a vast improvement:

> The aggressive shopkeepers had taken the whole city away from us and never kept to the limits of their thresholds. But you, Domitian, ordered our narrowed streets to expand and what had been but a path has now become a street. No longer do they chain wine bottles to the pillars in front of their shops, and no longer are officials forced to walk in the middle of the mud. No longer does the barber blindly draw his razor in a dense crowd, and no longer do the greasy fast-food shops take up the whole street. The barbers, bartenders, cooks, and butchers now keep to their own thresholds. Now Rome is a city again, whereas before it was just one big shop.
>
> Martial, *Epigrams* VII.61

Columns and Porticos

The column was one of the main features of Roman architecture. Sometimes a single column was used to support a statue; more often, columns were used to support the roofs or to form the entrance-porches of temples and other buildings.

From the idea of the porch, there developed the portico or long covered walk which afforded the citizens protection from sun and dust, while allowing them to enjoy the fresh air. In the shelter of the portico various activities took place. The Portico of Minucius was used as a corn-exchange; in another a vegetable market was held. In the porticos philosophers lectured, poets recited, schoolmasters held their classes, lawyers met their clients, entertainers performed, snacks were sold, and business deals were concluded. In fact, porticos became so common that it was eventually possible to walk from one end of the city to the other without coming out into the open at all!

According to one writer, porticos covered more than a quarter of the total area of the Campus Martius, the number of columns supporting them being about 2000. Halls built in the shelter of these housed wall-maps of Rome and the Roman world, exhibitions of wonders from the Far East, natural marvels such as a snake 23 yards or 21 meters long, and, in the Portico of Philippus, a display of wigs and the latest in ladies' hairstyles.

Exercise 24b

Take parts, read aloud, and translate:

SEXTUS: Quam dēfessus sum, Marce! Nam hodiē māne dormīre nōn poteram.
Tantus clāmor in viīs erat.

MARCUS: Quālem clāmōrem audīvistī? Ego certē nihil clāmōris audīvī.

SEXTUS: Quid? Nōnne audīvistī illōs canēs in viīs lātrantēs? Multās hōrās lātrābant. Numquam audīvī tantum strepitum. Audīvī etiam clāmōrem mul- 5
tōrum hominum quī per viās currēbant.

MARCUS: Quid clāmābant?

SEXTUS: Id audīre nōn poteram, nam omnēs simul clāmābant. Certē tamen īrātī
erant. Erat quoque strepitus plaustrōrum. Nōs in urbe heri plaustra nōn
vīdimus. Unde vēnērunt plaustra? 10

MARCUS: Interdiū nōn licet plaustra intrā urbem agere. Nocte igitur necesse est
labōrāre. Servī in urbem ferēbant cibum, vīnum, lapidēs —

SEXTUS: Cūr lapidēs intrā urbem tulērunt?

MARCUS: Caesar cōnstituit ingēns amphitheātrum in urbe aedificāre.

SEXTUS: Nōs illud aedificium vīdimus? 15

MARCUS: Heri illud cōnspexistī, ubi ad Forum cum patre meō dēscendēbāmus.
Heri nōn satis temporis erat id īnspicere quod pater domum festīnābat.
Sed mox amphitheātrum iterum vīsitābimus atque id īnspiciēmus. For-
tasse Eucleidēs nōs dūcet.

SEXTUS: Dum hoc mihi dīcis, multī hominēs in domum vēnērunt. Quī sunt? 20

MARCUS: Nōnne heri in urbe vīdistī multōs cīvēs post senātōrem sequentēs? Hic
erat patrōnus, illī erant clientēs. Pater meus est patrōnus multōrum
cīvium. Tū audīvistī clientēs domum intrantēs.

SEXTUS: Ēheu! Eucleidēs quoque intrāvit!

> **vīnum, -ī** (*n*), wine   **sequentēs,** following
> **īnspiciō, īnspicere** (3), **īnspexī, īnspectum,** to examine

Patrōnī were wealthy men who gave food or money to their dependents
(**clientēs**). The **clientēs** came to the patron's home early in the morning to
receive this dole and then escorted him to the Forum and performed other
services for him. Here is Juvenal's satirical comment:

> Now the meager dole sits on the outer edge of the threshold of the patron's
> house to be snatched up by the clients in their togas. But first the patron
> inspects each face, fearing that someone might come and claim his due
> under a false name. Once he recognizes you, you'll get your share.
>
> Juvenal, *Satires* I.95–99

Eucleides the Statistician

Marcus had always visualized himself showing Sextus around the city of Rome, but he should have realized that Cornelius would never allow Sextus and himself to wander around Rome unsupervised. If neither Cornelius nor Titus was free to act as guide, Eucleides was bound to be their companion. He certainly knew a lot; the trouble was, there was no stopping him.

"Rome," Eucleides was now saying in that affected Greek voice of his, "is built on seven hills, the most famous being the Capitol and the Palatine. By now, of course, it has far outstripped these petty limits. Augustus divided it into fourteen regions, which are in turn subdivided into 265 **vīcī** or wards. At the last census the population numbered 1,284,602, living in 1,797 **domūs** and 46,602 **īnsulae**."

"I can't see any islands!" complained Sextus, in all seriousness.

"**Īnsulae**," explained Eucleides, "are those ramshackle tenements where all the riff-raff live."

"And **Īnsula Feliculae** is the biggest in the world," said Marcus.

"There are," said Eucleides, "64 miles of streets, using your Roman measurements."

"Not very wide, are they?" commented Sextus.

"Maximum width according to *The Twelve Tables* was only 17 feet."

"And some of them are not even paved!" cried Sextus, peering along the dark tunnel they were now traversing between the **īnsulae**.

"Watch out!" yelled Marcus, pulling Sextus and Eucleides close to the wall to dodge a deluge of slops from a third-floor window.

"We'll have the law on you for that!" shouted Marcus up at the unseen law-breaker. But Eucleides, not anxious to linger bandying threats, hustled the boys off through the labyrinth of shadowy alleys.

Suddenly they emerged into the blinding sun of the open Forum.

"This," said Eucleides impressively, pointing to a massive column, "is the center of the universe, the *Golden Milestone*. Erected by Augustus, it bears upon it in letters of gilt bronze the distances to all the cities of the Empire."

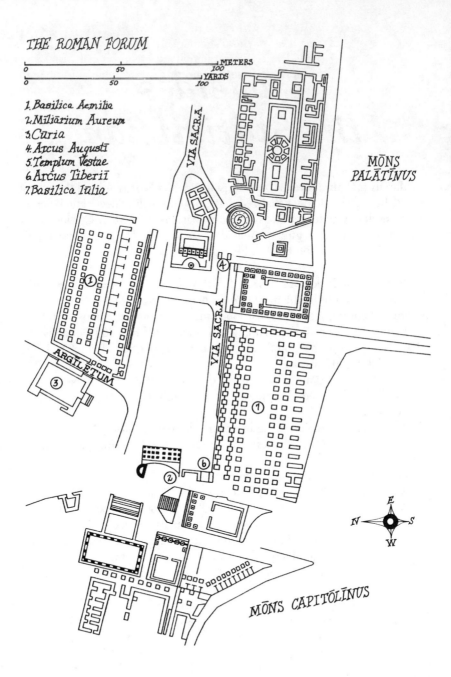

THE ROMAN FORUM

METERS
YARDS

1. Basilica Aemilia
2. Miliārium Aureum
3. Cūria
4. Arcus Augustī
5. Templum Vestae
6. Arcus Tiberiī
7. Basilica Iūlia

VIA SACRA

VIA SACRA

ARGILETUM

MŌNS
PALĀTĪNUS

MŌNS CAPITŌLĪNUS

But it was not the Golden Milestone the boys were looking at, nor was it the splendor of the Capitol behind them. They were gazing down at the **Forum Rōmānum** which glittered with marble and bronze and gold. Senators and businessmen with their slaves were hurrying in and out of the **basilicae** that flanked the Forum. The noise was deafening. Cries of sausage-sellers and pastry-vendors mingled with the uproar of every language under heaven. White toga and tunic jostled with all kinds of colors of outlandish garb.

Eucleides, sensing their preoccupation, was just pursing his lips to launch out on a lecture on the Forum; but Marcus and Sextus were off, scampering along the **Via Sacra**.

"Come and tell us what's going on here!" they shouted, running to the far end of the Forum where their attention had been caught by the feverish activity of an army of masons engaged, amidst mountains of rubble and building stone, in some mammoth task of demolition or construction—it was hard to tell which.

"The Emperor Nero—" began Eucleides breathlessly as he caught up with them.

"I know," said Marcus. "He's the one that set Rome on fire for fun."

"The Emperor Nero," Eucleides repeated, "on the space cleared of unsightly hovels by a quite accidental fire, built the wonderful **Domus Aurea**."

"And they're still working at it by the look of it!" said Sextus, grinning.

"No, you idiot!" said Marcus. "Vespasian and Titus pulled down parts of Nero's folly and are putting up things for the citizens of Rome to enjoy, baths, for instance, and—"

"And that terrific statue over there?" pointed Sextus.

"That was a statue of Nero himself," Marcus went on, "but Vespasian put rays around its head and made it into a statue of the sun-god."

"It is 118 feet high," began Eucleides, but his hearers were gone again, towards an immense building under construction.

"What's this?" they asked, as an exhausted Eucleides caught up with them.

"This is the **Amphitheātrum Flāvium**," he gasped. "The Emperor Titus is to dedicate it in June."

25
A Grim Lesson

Eucleidēs et puerī iam domum redierant. Post cēnam Cornēlius et Marcus et Sextus in ātriō sedēbant.

"Quid hodiē vīdistis, puerī?" inquit Cornēlius.

"Nihil nisi aedificia antīqua," respondit Marcus. "Nōs in urbem exīre volumus sōlī. Cūr nōn licet?" 5

Cui Cornēlius, "Est perīculōsum sine custōde exīre in viās huius urbis. Sunt multī hominēs scelestī quī bona cīvium arripiunt. Nōnnumquam hī hominēs cīvēs ipsōs necant. Vōbīs igitur nōn licet sine custōde exīre. Iam sērō est. Nunc necesse est vōbīs cubitum īre. Nōlīte cessāre sed īte statim!"

Puerī, labōre diēī dēfessī, simulac cubitum īvērunt, obdormīvērunt. 10

Postrīdiē māne Marcus in lectō suō iacēbat et dē Circō Maximō ita cōgitābat: "Quandō Circum Maximum vīsitābimus? Cūr pater meus nōs exīre vetat? Herī nūllōs hominēs scelestōs in urbe vīdī. Interdiū certē praedōnēs nōbīs nōn nocēbunt. Meum patrem, quod est senātor Rōmānus, praedōnēs timent. Nihil perīculī est." 15

Brevī tempore, ut Marcō vidēbātur, puerī ad Circum ībant. Mox mōlem ingentem Circī Maximī Marcus cōnspexit.

"Ecce!" clāmāvit Marcus. "Est Circus. Ubi intrāverimus, tandem aurīgās ipsōs spectābimus."

Subitō tamen in viam sē praecipitāvērunt trēs hominēs. 20

"Cavē illōs hominēs!" clāmāvit Sextus. "Illī certē nōs in domūs vīcīnās trahent et ibi nōs necābunt."

Sed frūstrā, nam Marcus, metū commōtus, postquam Sextum audīvit clāmantem, ad terram cecidit et iacēbat in lutō immōbilis.

"Eho!" clāmāvit ūnus ē praedōnibus. "Quō abīs, parvule? Quid est nōmen 25 tuum? Nōnne tū fīlius es senātōris? Nōnne nōmen tuum est Marcus Cornēlius?"

Cui Marcus, "Quid vultis, scelestī? Nihil pecūniae habeō. Nōlīte mē verberāre! Sī mihi nocueritis, pater meus certē vōs pūniet."

Sed interpellāvit praedō, "Tacē, puer! Tū es captīvus noster neque ad 30 patrem redībis. Nēmō nunc poterit tē servāre. Ipse enim tē necābō."

Tum praedō gladium strīnxit. Marcus stābat perterritus et, "Fer auxilium!" clāmāvit. "Fer auxilium!" Sed nēmō clāmōrem audīvit. Nēmō auxilium tulit. Marcus oculōs clausit et mortem exspectābat.

Nihil accidit. Oculōs aperuit. In lectō erat suō. Somnium modo fuerat. 35 Hodiē tamen domī manēre cōnstituit Marcus. Exīre nōluit.

atrium, -ī (n), ātiium, central room
in a Roman house
nisi, unless, except
sine (+ abl.), without
custōs, custōdis (m), guard
bona, bonōrum (n pl), goods, possessions
nōnnumquam, sometimes
postrīdiē, on the following day
iaceō (2), to lie, be lying down
noceō (2) (+ dat.), to harm
ut Marcō vidēbātur, as it seemed to Marcus, as Marcus thought
intrāverimus, we will have entered, we enter

metū commōtus, moved by fear, in a panic
terra, -ae (f), earth, ground
lutum, -ī (n), mud
parvulus, -a, -um, little
nocueritis, you will have harmed, you harm
neque, and . . . not
servō (1), to save
gladius, -ī (m), sword
oculus, -ī (m), eye
mors, mortis (f), death
domī, at home

arripiō, arripere (3), arripuī, arreptum, to snatch, seize
vetō, vetāre (1), vetuī, vetitum, to forbid
stringō, stringere (3), strīnxī, strictum, to draw
claudō, claudere (3), clausī, clausum, to shut
accidit, accidere (3), accidit, (it) happens
aperiō, aperīre (4), aperuī, apertum, to open
nōlō, nōlle (irreg.), nōluī, to be unwilling, not to wish, refuse

Exercise 25a

Respondē Latīnē:

1. Quid puerī in urbe hodiē vīdērunt?
2. Cūr nōn licet puerīs exīre in urbem sōlīs?
3. Quid faciunt hominēs scelestī in viīs urbis?
4. Quōcum puerīs licet exīre in urbem?
5. Quid Cornēlius puerōs statim facere iubet?
6. Quā dē rē Marcus postrīdiē in lectō cōgitābat?
7. Timetne Marcus interdiū in urbem exīre?
8. Praedōnēsne Marcō et Sextō interdiū nocēbunt?
9. Quem praedōnēs timēbunt?
10. Quō ībant puerī?
11. Quid Marcus cōnspexit?
12. Quī sē in viam praecipitāvērunt?
13. Quid fēcit Marcus postquam Sextum clāmantem audīvit?
14. Quid pater Marcī faciet sī praedōnēs Marcō nocuerint?
15. Cūr praedō gladium strīnxit?
16. Quis vēnit ubi Marcus clāmāvit?

Quōcum . . . ? With whom . . . ?

DEMONSTRATIVE ADJECTIVES: Hic and Ille

Look at the following sentences:

Ille tabellārius equōs vehementer incitāvit.

That *courier fiercely whipped
the horses on.*

Quis in illō aedificiō habitat?

Who *lives in that building over
there?*

Hī canēs lātrant modo.

These *dogs are only barking.*

Est perīculōsum in viās huius
urbis exīre.

It *is dangerous to go out into
the streets of this city.*

Sextus, hīs clāmōribus et hōc
strepitū excitātus, dormīre
nōn poterat.

Roused by these *shouts and this
noise, Sextus could not sleep.*

You will see from the above examples that both hic and ille are used to
point out someone or something. Hic points to someone or something near
at hand or near in time, while ille points to someone or something further
away or "over there" or distant in time.

Here is a table showing all the cases of hic ("this," "these") and ille
("that," "those") in masculine, feminine, and neuter genders:

Number Case	Masc.	Fem.	Neut.	Masc.	Fem.	Neut.
Singular						
Nominative	hic	haec	hoc	ille	illa	illud
Genitive	huius	huius	huius	illīus	illīus	illīus
Dative	huic	huic	huic	illī	illī	illī
Accusative	hunc	hanc	hoc	illum	illam	illud
Ablative	hōc	hāc	hōc	illō	illā	illō
Plural						
Nominative	hī	hae	haec	illī	illae	illa
Genitive	hōrum	hārum	hōrum	illōrum	illārum	illōrum
Dative	hīs	hīs	hīs	illīs	illīs	illīs
Accusative	hōs	hās	haec	illōs	illās	illa
Ablative	hīs	hīs	hīs	illīs	illīs	illīs

Be sure you know all of the above forms.

Exercise 25b

Using story 25 as a guide, give the Latin for:

1. It is dangerous to go out into the streets of this city.
2. Why does my father forbid us to visit the Circus Maximus?
3. Watch out for those men!
4. You are our prisoner and no one will be able to save you.

Exercise 25c

Choose the proper form of **hic** or **ille** to fill each blank, and then read the sentence aloud and translate:

1. Cornēliī in _____ vīllā habitant.
2. "Spectāte _____ arcum, puerī!" clāmāvit Eucleidēs.
3. Ōlim _____ puellae in agrīs ambulābant.
4. Vīlicus cibum _____ servō nōn dabit.
5. "Vīdistīne _____ aedificium, Marce?" inquit Sextus.
6. Raeda _____ mercātōris prope tabernam manet.
7. Māne _____ canēs ferōciter lātrābant.
8. Bona _____ rūsticōrum in raedā erant.
9. Ūnus ex _____ praedōnibus gladium strīnxit.
10. Nōbīs _____ arborēs ascendere nōn licet.
11. _____ rem explicāre nōn possum.
12. _____ strepitus Marcum nōn excitāvit.

Exercise 25d

Read aloud and translate:

1. Hic puer in hāc viā, ille puer in illā viā habitat.
2. Illa puella in hāc vīllā habitat; hī puerī in illā vīllā habitant.
3. Nōnne illud aedificium mox ad terram cadet?
4. Sī in hāc caupōnā pernoctābimus, hic caupō nōbīs certē nocēbit.
5. Illī praedōnēs illōs viātōrēs sub hīs arboribus petunt.
6. Quandō illī servī haec onera in vīllam portābunt?
7. Nōlī illud plaustrum in hanc urbem interdiū agere!
8. Huic puerō multa dabimus, illī nihil.
9. Hīs rūsticīs licēbit agrōs huius vīllae colere.
10. Huic senātōrī ad Cūriam in lectīcā redīre necesse erat.
11. Illī aedificiō appropinquāre perīculōsum est, nam mūrī sunt īnfirmī.
12. Ūnus ex hīs praedōnibus aliquid illī servō dīcēbat.

VERBS: *Future Perfect Tense*

Look at these sentences:

Ubi **intrāverimus,** tandem aurīgās ipsōs spectābimus.
When we enter (**will have entered, have entered**), *we will finally watch the charioteers themselves.*
Sī mihi **nocueritis,** pater meus certē vōs pūniet.
If you harm (**will have harmed**) *me, my father will surely punish you.*

The verbs in boldface above are in the *future perfect tense.* The future perfect tense is used to express an action in the future which will be completed before another action will begin. Note that the Latin future perfect is often best translated by the present tense in English.

The endings of the future perfect tense are the same for *all* Latin verbs:

1 *-erō*	1 *-erimus*
Singular 2 *-eris*	Plural 2 *-eritis*
3 *-erit*	3 *-erint*

Note that, except for the third person plural, these endings are the same as the forms of the future tense of **esse.** These endings are added to the perfect stem, which is found by dropping the **-ī** from the end of the third principal part of the verb, e.g., **nocuī,** stem **nocu-.**

1 nocu**erō**	1 nocu**erimus**
Singular 2 nocu**eris**	Plural 2 nocu**eritis**
3 nocu**erit**	3 nocu**erint**

Exercise 25e

Read aloud and translate:

1. Sī illud baculum coniēceris, hī canēs ferōciter lātrābunt.
2. Ubi ad Portam Capēnam advēnerimus, ē raedā dēscendēmus.
3. Sī equī raedam ē fossā extrāxerint, Cornēliī ad urbem iter facere poterunt.
4. Nisi caupō alium lectum in cubiculum mōverit, Aurēlia ibi dormīre nōlet.
5. Crās puerī, ubi surrēxerint, strepitum plaustrōrum audient.

moveō, movēre (2), **mōvī, mōtum,** to move

26
A Visit to the Races

Chariot-racing (**lūdī circēnsēs**) was perhaps the most popular spectacle in ancient Rome. It was held in the **Circus Maximus**, a huge open-air stadium in the valley between the Palatine and the Aventine hills. It could hold about 200,000 spectators, seated in tiers around the long course (**arēna**).

It has been estimated that at one time some 90 holidays (**fēriae**) were given over to games at public expense. On these days the citizens were "celebrating a holiday" (**fēriātī**).

A barrier (**spīna**) ran down the center of the course, and the chariots (**quadrīgae**), each pulled by four horses, had to complete seven laps, about five miles or eight kilometers in all. Fouling was permitted, and collisions were frequent, especially at the turning posts (**mētae**). A race began when the Emperor or presiding official gave the signal (**signum**) by dropping a white cloth (**mappa**).

The charioteers, some of whom won great popularity and very high salaries, were employed by four companies (**factiōnēs**), each with its own color—the "Reds" (**russātī**), the "Whites" (**albātī**), the "Greens" (**prasinī**), and the "Blues" (**venetī**). Rival groups of spectators were accustomed to show their support (**favēre**) for each color vociferously.

One charioteer we hear about, Gaius Apuleius Diocles, drove chariots for the Red Stable for twenty-four years, ran 4,257 starts, and won 1,462 victories.

No wonder Marcus, Cornelia, and Sextus are eager to go to the races! As we return to our story, three days after the Cornelii arrived in Rome, Sextus is sitting alone when suddenly Marcus rushes in.

MARCUS: Sexte! Sexte! Hodiē nōbīs licet ad lūdōs circēnsēs īre. Eucleidēs mē et tē et Cornēliam ad Circum dūcet.
SEXTUS: Lūdōs circēnsēs amō. Sed nōnne Circus clausus erit?
MARCUS: Minimē! Circus nōn erit clausus, nam hodiē cīvēs omnēs fēriātī sunt. Viae erunt plēnae hominum. Virī, mulierēs, 5 līberī Circum celerrimē petent.
SEXTUS: Sed cūr nōn nunc discēdimus? Ego sum iam parātus.
MARCUS: Simulac Cornēlia ē somnō surrēxerit, statim ībimus.

mulier, mulieris (*f*), woman

(Much to the boys' disgust, Cornelia was rather late in waking up from her siesta, but soon they were all ready to leave.)

85

EUCLEIDĒS: Agite! Iam tandem ad Circum īre tempus est. Estisne parātī, puerī? Esne parāta, Cornēlia?   10

(Eucleides takes Cornelia and the boys quickly through the streets; they can now hear the noise of the Circus crowds.)

EUCLEIDĒS: Iam ā Circō nōn procul absumus. Nōnne strepitum audītis? Ecce! Omnēs ad Circum festīnant. Brevī tempore nōs ipsī intrābimus.

(They enter the Circus.)

CORNĒLIA: Quam ingēns est turba hominum! Tōtus Circus est plēnus spectātōrum.   15

EUCLEIDĒS: Ita vērō! Semper multī spectātōrēs in Circō sunt. Hīc cōnsīdēmus?

MARCUS: Minimē! Prope arēnam sedēre necesse est quod ibi omnia vidēre poterimus.

tōtus, -a, -um, all, the whole

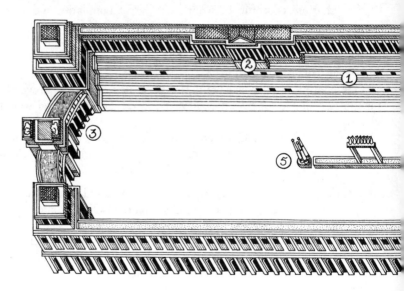

EUCLEIDĒS:	At prope arēnam sedēre perīculōsum est. Pater vester multa	20
	dē perīculō dīxit.	
MARCUS:	Nihil perīculī est, nam Titus, patruus meus, cum amīcīs	
	prope arēnam sedēre solet.	
SEXTUS:	Ecce! Caesar ipse iam surrēxit; signum dare parat. Ego	
	russātīs favēbō.	25
MARCUS:	Ego albātīs.	
CORNĒLIA:	Ego venetīs.	
MARCUS:	Ecce! Mappa! Signum est!	
CORNĒLIA:	Quam ferōciter equōs verberant illī aurīgae! Quam celeriter	
	equōs agunt! Quam temerāriī sunt! Nōnne mortem timent?	30
SEXTUS:	Ecce! Russātus meus certē victor erit, nam equōs magnā	
	arte agit.	

faveō, favēre (2), **fāvī, fautum** (+ *dat.*), to favor, support

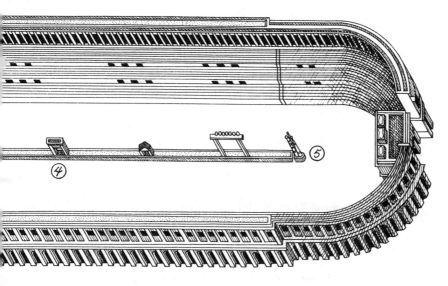

1. *Spectators' seats*
2. *Emperor's and distinguished guests' seats*
3. *Carceres (stalls)*
4. *Spina (low platform)*
5. *Metae (turning posts)*

MARCUS:	Ō mē miserum! Aurīga meus equōs dēvertit. Cavē mētam! Cavē mētam! Esne sēmisomnus, fatue? Cūr mētam nōn vītāvistī? 35
CORNĒLIA:	Ēheu! Ille aurīga cecidit. In arēnā iacet. Estne mortuus?
SEXTUS:	Minimē! Minimē! Ecce! Animum recuperāvit. Iam surgit.
CORNĒLIA:	Audīvistisne clāmōrēs hōrum spectātōrum? Magnā vōce nōmina aurīgārum et equōrum semper clāmant! Undique ingēns est strepitus! Tantum strepitum ego numquam au- 40 dīvī.
MARCUS:	Russātī hanc victōriam habent, sed mox etiam albātī habēbunt victōriam. Glōria albātōrum erit immortālis.
EUCLEIDĒS:	Hoc fortasse accidet, sed Caligula ipse, ut dīcunt, prasinōs amābat.

dēvertō, dēvertere (3), dēvertī, dēversum, to turn aside

(They watch a few more races, but it is not Marcus' lucky day. Eucleides becomes a little anxious as it grows later. He had been caught once before in a crush at the gates.)

EUCLEIDĒS: Iam sērō est. Nunc domum redībimus.

SEXTUS: Nōndum tempus est domum redīre. Ecce! Aurīgae habēnās sūmpsērunt et signum exspectant.

EUCLEIDĒS: Nisi mox discēdēmus, turbam ingentem vītāre nōn poterimus. Agite! Domum!

PREFIXES: Compound Verbs

Compare the following sentences:

1. Equī raedam **trahunt**.
   The horses **pull** *the coach.*
2. Servī lectum **ferēbant**.
   The slaves **were carrying** *the bed.*

1. Equī raedam **extrahunt**.
   The horses **pull out** *the coach.*
2. Servī lectum **referēbant**.
   The slaves **were carrying back** *the bed.*

In the right-hand column a prefix has been added to the beginning of the verb to give it a more specific meaning. Verbs with prefixes attached to them are called *compound verbs*. Common prefixes are:

ab-, abs-, ā-, away, from
ad-, towards, to
circum-, around
con-, along with, together (or simply to emphasize)
dē-, down, down from
dis-, dī-, apart, in different directions
ex-, ē-, out, out of
in-, into, in, on

inter-, between
per-, through (or simply to emphasize)
prae-, in front, ahead
praeter-, past, beyond
prō-, prōd-, forward
re-, red-, back, again
sub-, under, below
trāns-, trā- across

Note that many of these are common prepositions.

Be sure to learn these prefixes thoroughly.

Exercise 26a

Give the meaning of:

1. abesse, adesse, inesse, praeesse, subesse, interesse.
2. abīre, adīre, praeterīre, trānsīre, redīre, exīre, inīre, praeīre, subīre, circumīre.
3. referre, trānsferre, cōnferre, īnferre, praeferre, dēferre.
4. discēdere, excēdere, incēdere, recēdere, prōcēdere, intercēdere, praecēdere.

   cēdo, cēdere (3), **cessī, cessum,** to come, go

Exercise 26b

Read aloud and translate:

1. Pater līberōs ē vīllā ēdūxit et trāns viam trādūxit.
2. Cornēlius Eucleidem iussit līberōs abdūcere.
3. Eucleidēs līberōs ad hortum redūxit.
4. Servī togās et tunicās in cistīs repōnunt.
5. Ubi ad Portam Capēnam veniunt, servī onera dēpōnunt.

6. Ubi plaustrum invēnit, stercus remōvit et corpus extraxit.
7. Cornēliī Rōmam heri advēnērunt.
8. Homō per viam it. Mox viam transībit et ad vīllam redībit.
9. Ubi urbem intrāmus, necesse est Aquam Marciam subīre.
10. Puerī Circum relīquērunt et Palātīnum circumiērunt.
11. Nihil clāmōris, nihil strepitūs ad Marcum pervēnerat.
12. Puerōs, quod praecurrēbant, identidem revocābat Cornēlius.

Honorary Inscription

P. Aelius, Marī Rogātī fil(ius), Gutta Calpurniānus equīs hīs vīcī in factiōne venetā: Germinātōre n(igrō) Ā(frō) LXXXXII, Silvānō r(ūfō) Āf(rō) CV, Nitid(ō) gil(vō) Āf(rō) LII, Saxōne n(igrō) Āf(rō) LX, et vīcī praemia m(aiōra) L̄ I, X̄L̄ IX, X̄X̄X̄ XVII.

I, Publius Aelius Gutta Calpurnianus, son of Marius Rogatus, won for the Blue stable with the following horses: Germinator, African black, 92 (times); Silvanus, African chestnut, 105 (times); Glossy, African sorrel, 52 (times); Saxon, African black, 60 (times); and I won major purses of 50,000 sesterces (1), of 40,000 sesterces (9), and of 30,000 sesterces (17).

Sepulchral Inscription

D. M. Epaphrodītus agitātor f(actiōnis) r(ussātae), vīc(it) CLXXVIII, et ad purpureum līber(ātus) vīc(it) VIII. Beia Felicula f(ēcit) coniugī suō b(ene) merentī.

To the deified spirits (of) Epaphroditus, driver for the Red stable; he won 178 (times), and after being manumitted to the Purples he won 8 (times). Beia Felicula made (this monument) for her deserving husband.

Curses against Charioteers and Their Horses

Adiūrō tē daemōn quīcumque es et dēmandō tibi ex hāc hōrā ex hāc diē ex hōc mōmentō, ut equōs Prasinī et Albī cruciēs occīdās, et agitātōrēs Clārum et Fēlīcem et Prīmulum et Rōmānum occīdās collīdās, neque spīritum illīs relinquās.

I adjure you, demon, whoever you are, and I ask of you from this hour, from this day, from this moment, that you torture and kill the horses of the Green and the White, and that you kill and smash their drivers Clarus and Felix and Primulus and Romanus, and leave no breath in them.

Versiculī: "Medea," pages 103–105.

Word Study VII

Prefixes

Knowledge of Latin prefixes will help not only with the meanings of Latin compound verbs but also with the meanings of many English words derived from them. For example, when the Latin simple verb **portāre** is combined with various prefixes, the resulting compound verbs provide English with several words, e.g.:

deport (from **dēportāre**)   report (from **reportāre**)
export (from **exportāre**)   transport (from **trānsportāre**)

Relying on your knowledge of prefixes, can you tell the meaning of each of the English words above?

Some English words are derived from the infinitive stem of the Latin compound verb, e.g., *transport* (from **trānsportāre**). Others are derived from the supine stem, e.g., *transportation* (from **trānsportātum**). (For the suffix *-tion* see Word Study VI.)

Exercise 1

After each Latin simple verb below is a group of English verbs which are derived from Latin compounds of that simple verb. (The Latin compound verbs are in parentheses.) Give the meaning of each English verb:

dūcō, dūcere (3), dūxī, ductum

1. to conduct (**condūcere**)
2. to induct (**indūcere**)
3. to deduct (**dēdūcere**)
4. to reduce (**redūcere**)
5. to produce (**prōdūcere**)
6. to adduce (**addūcere**)

pōnō, pōnere (3), posuī positum

1. to propose (**prōpōnere**)
2. to dispose (**dispōnere**)
3. to expose (**expōnere**)
4. to depose (**dēpōnere**)
5. to transpose (**trānspōnere**)
6. to deposit (**dēpōnere**)

cēdō, cēdere (3), cessī, cessum

1. to precede (**praecēdere**)
2. to recede (**recēdere**)
3. to intercede (**intercēdere**)

variant spelling:
4. to proceed (**prōcēdere**)
5. to exceed (**excēdere**)

Note that **cēdere** can also mean *to yield*. From this meaning come the following English derivatives:

6. to cede (**cēdere**)
7. to concede (**concēdere**)

fero, ferre (*Irreg.*), **tulī, lātum**

1. to refer (**referre**)
2. to infer (**īnferre**)
3. to defer (**dēferre**)
4. to transfer (**trānsferre**)
5. to confer (**cōnferre**)
6. to relate (**referre**)

Exercise 2

Give the infinitive of the Latin compound verb from which each of the following English nouns is derived. Use each English noun in a sentence which illustrates its meaning:

1. disposition
2. proponent
3. recess
4. inference
5. product
6. exposition
7. relation
8. procession
9. conference
10. precedent
11. translator
12. concession
13. deduction
14. referee
15. reference

Exercise 3

Each adjective in the pool below is derived from a Latin compound verb. Choose an adjective to fill each blank and give the Latin compound verb from which it is derived:

1. Eucleides provided an atmosphere for the boys that would lead them to learn. The atmosphere was _____ to learning.
2. The slave-woman, Syra, was shy and preferred not to socialize with the other slaves. Syra had a _____ personality.
3. Although the horses tried to pull the carriage out, their efforts brought forth no results. Their efforts were not _____.
4. Some masters treat their slaves with violence which goes beyond reasonable limits. Their use of violence is _____.
5. Davus was not unhappy, but he was not as happy as he might have been if he were not a slave. Davus enjoyed _____ happiness.
6. When Cornelius entered a shop, the merchant left the other customers and helped him immediately. Cornelius received _____ treatment.
7. After he considered all of the evidence, the overseer was certain which slave stole the money. The overseer used _____ reasoning to come to his conclusion.
8. When the emperor went by, all the citizens bowed respectfully. The emperor was greeted in a _____ manner.

relative	deferential	recessive	conducive
productive	excessive	preferential	deductive

93

Latin Abbreviations in English

Many abbreviations used in English are actually abbreviations of Latin words. For example, the common abbreviations for morning and afternoon, A.M. and P.M., stand for the Latin phrases **ante merīdiem** (*before noon*) and **post merīdiem** (*after noon*).

Exercise 4

With the aid of an English dictionary, give the full Latin words for the following abbreviations and explain how each is used in English:

1.	etc.	4.	i.e.	7.	ad lib.	10.	et al.
2.	A.D.	5.	e.g.	8.	vs.	11.	q.v.
3.	P.S.	6.	N.B.	9.	cf.	12.	℞

Exercise 5

Replace the words in italics with abbreviations chosen from the list in Exercise 4 above:

1. The senators discussed the most critical problems first, *for example*, the revolt in Judea.
2. Titus was known for his ability to *speak at will* on almost any subject.
3. The eruption of Vesuvius occurred in *the year of our Lord* 79.
4. Titus pointed out the Curia, the Arch of Tiberius, *and the rest*, as they passed them.
5. The announcement of the chariot race read, "Reds *against* Blues."
6. Eucleides said that they would return early, *that is*, before the eleventh hour.
7. At the bottom of the letter Cornelius added an *afterthought*.
8. Cornelius had invited Titus, Messala, *and others*, to a dinner-party.
9. The abbreviation "B.C." is used to give dates before the birth of Christ. (*Compare* the abbreviation "A.D.")
10. A sign near the Porta Capena read, "*Note well:* It is forbidden to drive wagons or carriages within the city during the day."
11. "*Take this*" was written at the bottom of the doctor's prescription.
12. "*Which see*" is written after a word or topic which needs further explanation, and it directs the reader to find such explanation elsewhere in the book.

Find examples of Latin abbreviations in textbooks, newspapers, or magazines and bring them to class.

Review VI

Exercise VIa

From the list at the right select appropriate words to go with each of
the following nouns. Give alternatives where requested.

1. _____ diem
2. _____ arbore
3. _____ lutum
4. _____ or _____ or _____ diēs
5. _____ fēminam
6. _____ terrās
7. _____ or _____ mandātō
8. _____ terra
9. _____ or _____ oculō
10. _____ arcuum
11. _____ somnia
12. _____ rīsū
13. _____ vōcum
14. _____ diē
15. _____ or _____ or _____ manūs
16. _____ capitum
17. _____ custōs
18. _____ or_____ reī
19. _____ or _____ or _____ tabernae
20. _____ rēbus
21. _____ caupōnī
22. _____ or _____ servī
23. _____ or _____ praedōnēs
24. _____ custōdum

hōs
hīs
hoc
huic
hunc
hōc
hās
huius
hārum
hāc
hic
hī
hanc
hae
haec
hōrum

Exercise VIb

From the pool of words below, choose an adjective to go with each noun
in Exercise VIa above. Give the noun with the adjective in its proper
form to modify the noun.

bonus, -a, -um	īrātus, -a, -um	parvulus, -a, -um
brevis, -is, -e	longus, -a, -um	pūrus, -a, -um
dēfessus, -a, -um	magnus, -a, -um	scelestus, -a, -um
prīmus, -a, -um	multī, -ae, -a	sēmisomnus, -a, -um
īnfirmus, -a, -um	novus, -a, -um	sordidus, -a, -um
ingēns, ingentis	omnis, -is, -e	vester, vestra, vestrum

Exercise VIc

Choose the correct form of the two choices in parentheses, read the sentence aloud, and translate it:

1. Sextus (illī, illō) arcuī appropinquāvit.
2. Mīles (illum, illud) gladium strīnxit.
3. Herculēs (illā, illō) manū Cerberum ex Īnferīs extrāxit.
4. Lātrātus (illum, illōrum) canum puerōs dormientēs excitāvit.
5. Cornēliī (illī, illō) diē Rōmam advēnērunt.

Exercise VId

Read the passage below and answer, in English, the questions that follow:

Porsinna, rēx Clūsīnōrum, urbem Rōmam iam diū obsidēbat. Rōmānī igitur, quod cibum in urbem afferre nōn poterant, fame perībant. Tum adulēscēns quīdam Rōmānus, Gāius Mūcius nōmine, quī cīvēs suōs servāre volēbat, Porsinnam necāre cōnstituit.

Itaque Mūcius, ubi Cūriam intrāvit, senātōribus, "Tiberim transīre," inquit, 5
"et castra hostium intrāre volō. Ibi Porsinnam petam et, sī dī adiuvābunt, eum necābō."

Cui senātōrēs, "Sī hoc facere vīs, nōs tē nōn vetāmus." Laetus domum rediit Mūcius. Gladium sūmpsit et intrā vestēs cēlāvit. Trāns Tiberim festīnāvit et in castra hostium clam intrāvit. Ibi magnam multitūdinem mīlitum vīdit. 10
Ad mēnsam sedēbant duo hominēs. Alter pecūniam mīlitibus dabat, alter spectābat. Sēcum cogitābat Mūcius, "Uter est rēx? Nōnne is est quī omnia facit? Illum necābō." Gladium strīnxit. Hominem necāvit. Stupuit turba adstantium. Ex castrīs paene effūgerat Mūcius cum custōdēs rēgis eum comprehendērunt. "Ō sceleste!" inquiunt. "Cūr scrībam rēgis necāvistī?" 15

"At rēgem," inquit Mūcius, "necāre voluī."

Rēx, ubi hoc audīvit, clāmāvit, "Ego tē gravissimē pūniam."

Superbē respondit Mūcius, "Cīvis sum Rōmānus. Mē Gāium Mūcium vocant. Cīvēs Rōmānī, quī magnam glōriam petunt, poenās nōn timent."

Forte Mūcius tum stābat prope ignem quī in altāribus erat. Subitō dextram 20
manum in ignem iniēcit. Statim rēx surrēxit et iussit custōdēs virum ab igne trahere. "Quamquam," inquit, "hostis es, tamen, quod vir fortissimus es, tē ad cīvēs tuōs iam remittō."

Postquam Mūcius Rōmam rediit, rem tōtam cīvibus narrāvit. Illī nōn modo Mūcium laudābant sed, quod iam sinistram modo manum habēbat, cognōmen 25
eī dedērunt Scaevolam.

rēx, rēgis (m), king
fame perīre, to die of hunger
adulēscēns, adulēscentis (m), young man
castra, -ōrum (n pl), camp
hostis, hostis (m), enemy
dī, deōrum (m pl), the gods
vestis, vestis (f), garment
clam, secretly
mēnsa, -ae (f), table
Uter . . . ? Utra . . . ?
 Utrum . . . ? Which . . . ?
 (of two)

paene, almost
scrība, -ae (m), clerk
gravissimē, very seriously
superbē, proudly
poena, -ae (f), punishment
forte, by chance
ignis, ignis (m), fire
altāria, altārium (n pl), altar
dexter, dextra, dextrum, right
fortissimus, -a, -um, very brave
sinister, sinistra, sinistrum, left
cognōmen, cognōminis (n), nick-name, surname

obsideō, obsidēre (2), obsēdī, obsessum, to besiege
afferō, afferre (irreg.), attulī, allātum, to carry towards, bring
comprehendō, comprehendere (3), comprehendī, comprehēnsum, to seize, arrest
stupeō, stupēre (2), stupuī, to be astonished

1. What was the effect of King Porsinna's siege of Rome?
2. Who decided to kill Porsinna? Why?
3. What four things did he propose to do?
4. Did the senators grant permission? Quote the Latin words which support your answer.
5. Quote two words that show that Mucius was disguising his intentions as he went about his mission.
6. What was each of the two men at the table doing?
7. What made Mucius decide which of the two was the king?
8. Whom did the guards tell him he had killed?
9. Quote and translate the words which express the king's first reaction.
10. What boast did Mucius make about himself?
11. What boast did Mucius make about his fellow citizens?
12. What did he do to show he was not afraid?
13. What order did the king give the guards?
14. What reason did the king give for sending Mucius home?
15. Translate the clause **quod iam sinistram modo manum habēbat.**
16. What do you think is the meaning of the nickname "Scaevola"?

Exercise VIe

Give the appropriate future perfect form of each verb in parentheses, read the sentence aloud, and translate:

1. "Sī ego ad Cūriam sērō (advenīre), senātōrēs īrātī erunt," cōgitābat Cornēlius.
2. Ubi pater manūs (lavāre) et togam pūram (induere), ad Cūriam statim ībit.
3. "Nisi tū pecūniam nōbīs (dare), tē certē necābō," clāmāvit praedō.
4. Illōs praedōnēs, sī Marcō (nocēre), Cornēlius certē pūniet.
5. "Ubi fābulam mīlitis (audīre), pater, statim cubitum ībimus," inquit Marcus.

Exercise VIf

Give the requested forms of the following verbs in the present, imperfect, future, perfect, pluperfect, and future perfect tenses:

	Present	Imperfect	Future	Perfect	Pluperfect	Future Perfect
1. vetāre (1st pl.)						
2. aperīre (3rd pl.)						
3. stertere (2nd pl.)						
4. esse (3rd sing.)						
5. emō (3rd sing.)						
6. ferre (2nd sing.)						
7. arripere (1st sing.)						
8. docēre (1st sing.)						
9. posse (2nd sing.)						
10. velle (1st pl.)						

98

VERSICULĪ

10 Arrival at the Inn
(after Chapter 17)

Caupōnam petimus caupōque recēpit obēsus.
  "Hīc bene dormītur," dīcit, inīre iubēns.

recēpit, (he) welcomed (us)
bene dormītur, you'll sleep well
dīcō, dīcere (3), to say
ineō, inīre (*irreg.*), to come in
iubēns, bidding (us)

11 Murder
(after Chapter 20)

(i)

Septimus in somnō tē cōnspicit, Aule, necātum.
  Crās (ēheu!) in plaustrō trīste cadāver erit.

(ii)

"Fer, comes, auxilium!" clāmāvī, "Septime." Sed tū,
  "Somnia," dīxistī, "maesta fuēre modo."
Nunc, quod non illīs potuistī crēdere verbīs,
  nunc quaere in faenō corpus, amīce, meum!

(iii)

Cūr Marcus cubitum īre timet vigilatque etiam nunc?
  Quod puerum timidum fābula mīra movet.

erit, (it) will be
trīste cadāver, a wretched corpse
comes, comitis (*m/f*), companion
maestus, -a, -um, sad
fuēre = **fuērunt**
potuistī, you were able
illīs crēdere verbīs, to believe those words
quaerō, quaerere (3), **quaesīvī, quaesītum,** to look for
faenum, -ī (*n*), hay
mīrus, -a, -um, wonderful, strange

12 Procrustes
(after Chapter 23)

The young hero Theseus is making his way to Athens. During his journey, he has met and overcome many giants, paying them in kind for their evil ways. He is almost to the city when he encounters the last of the giants, Procrustes. The name means "Stretcher." Why "Stretcher"? This the story reveals.

Longum iter est calidusque diēs. Stetit ille. Sinistrā
    parte videt magnam nōn procul inde domum.
"Rēx latrōnum habitat caupō-ne benignus in illā?"
    sē rogat. It propius. Iānua aperta manet.
In quā verba legit. "Salvē,"—sīc scrībitur—"hospes.   5
    Hīc bene dormītur. Hūc et adīre tibi—
sōlus sī veniēs—licet, hīc carnemque parātam
    sūmere et in lectō pōnere membra meō."
Intrāvit Thēseus. Carnem cōnsūmere multam
    audet et in lectō pōnere membra sua.   10
Mox obdormīvit. Parva est mora. Somnia vīdit:
    audent magna ambōs mōnstra tenēre pedēs!
Sollicitus somnīs sēsē excitat. Ecce, super sē
    cōnspexit hostem stāre minante manū.
Tālia quī magnā reprehendit vōce, "Viātor,   15
    sat iam audēs lectī, iam sat habēre cibī.
Quod dēbētur adest nōbīs iam solvere tempus!"
    Cui Thēseus, "Quid mē solvere, amīce, iubēs?"
"Tālia praebēbis," dīxit, "lūdibria nōbīs
    quālia iam hīc omnēs quī iacuēre prius.   20
Nam quōs inveniō prō lectīs esse minōrēs
    illōrum extendet māchina membra potēns.
Sed quī longa nimis praebēbit membra, necesse est
    aut illī caput aut ense secāre pedēs.
Haec in tē faciam!" dīxit gladiumque levābat.   25
    Quem Thēseus petiit corripuitque manū.
Nec longum sequitur certāmen membraque fiunt
    caupōnis lectīs ōcius apta suīs.

stō, stāre (1), stetī statum, to stand

sinister, sinistra, sinistrum, left (as
   opposed to right)

inde, from there

rēx, rēgis (m), king

latrō, latrōnis (m), thief

-ne, or

propius, nearer, closer

apertus, -a, -um, open

5 verbum, -ī (n), word

sīc scrībitur, thus it is written

bene dormītur, you'll sleep well

adeō, adīre (irreg.), adiī, aditum,
   to approach

carō, carnis (f), meat

membrum, -ī (n), limb

0 audeō, audēre (2), ausus sum,
   to dare

parvus, -a, -um, small, short

mora, -ae (f), delay, passage of
   time

ambō, -ae, -ō, both

mōnstrum, -ī (n), monster

pēs, pedis (m), foot

super (+ acc.), above

4 hostis, -is (m), enemy

minante manū, with threatening
   hand

quod dēbētur, what you owe

solvō, solvere (3), solvī, solūtum,
   to pay

tālia . . . quālia, such . . . as

praebeō (2), to offer, provide

lūdibrium, -ī (n), amusement, fun

20 iaceō (2), to lie, recline
   (iacuēre = iacuērunt)

prius, before

prō (+ abl.), in relation to

minōrēs, smaller, shorter

māchina, -ae (f), machine

potēns, potentis, powerful

nimis, too

illī (dat.), for, of that (person)

caput, capitis (n), head

ensis, ensis (m), sword

secō, secāre (1), secuī, sectum,
   to cut

25 haec, these things

gladius, -ī (m), sword

levō (1), to raise

petiit = petīvit

corripiō, corripere (3), corripuī,
   correptum, to grab hold of, seize

sequitur, (it) follows

certāmen, certāminis (n), struggle,
   contest

fiunt, (they) become, are made

ōcius, quickly

aptus, -a, -um, fitted to, of a
   suitable length for (+ dat.)

Answer in Latin or English the following questions on Versiculī 12 (Procrustes):

1. Why do you think Theseus stopped (line 1)?
2. Where did he see a house?
3. What two questions does he ask himself (line 3)?
4. Is the house inviting (line 4)? How so?
5. What does the house promise (line 6)?
6. What restriction does the house place on its hospitality (line 7)?
7. What two things can a guest do in the house (lines 7–8)?
8. What four things does Theseus proceed to do (lines 9–11)?
9. What does he see in his dream (line 12)?
10. What does he see when he wakes up?
11. According to the speaker in line 16, of what two things has Theseus had enough?
12. What does Procrustes say it is time to do now (line 17)?
13. What must Theseus offer in payment for his food and rest (lines 19–20)?
14. What does Procrustes do with short people (lines 21–22)?
15. What does he do with people who are too tall (lines 23–24)?
16. Judging from line 25, were Theseus' limbs too short or too long?
17. What does Theseus do when Procrustes attacks him (line 26)?
18. What does Theseus do to Procrustes (lines 27–28)?

BONUS QUESTION: What clause early in the poem foreshadows trouble?

13 Medea
(after Chapter 26)

In order to win back the kingdom which was his by right, Jason was told to sail to
the far land of Colchis and bring back the Golden Fleece which was guarded by a
great and ever-watchful serpent. There the king, Aeëtes by name, was very unwilling
to part with his priceless treasure and laid upon Jason a seemingly impossible task.
He was to take two fire-breathing bulls, plough a field with them, and sow there a
dragon's teeth, from which would immediately spring a nation of warriors bent on
murdering him. King Aeëtes thought he had baffled Jason's attempt. Surely he would
never face such a trial, or if he did there could be no doubt how things would turn
out. But Aeëtes reckoned without the goddess of love, who put into his daughter's
heart a fierce passion for the brave stranger. This daughter, Medea, was a sorceress
and knew the secret powers of many herbs and spells. She smeared Jason with a
magic ointment which provided an effective antidote to the bulls' fiery breath and
told him, when the warriors sprang up to kill him, to throw a stone into their midst.
They would be sure to blame one another and begin a fight which would end in
their deaths at each other's hands. She used her magic also to charm the serpent
and get away safely with Jason and the fleece in the good ship Argo.

Aeētae postquam audīvit crūdēlia verba
　　hērōs, (heu!) stupuit conticuitque diū.
Verba patris nec nōn audīvit fīlia; nocte
　　quae vēnit mediā, fīdaque verba dedit:
"Quod iubeō sī crās faciēs, et vīvus abīre　　　　　　　5
　　aurea et incolumis vellera habēre potes.
Sed quamquam secūrus eris, simulāre timōrem
　　dēbēbis multum fātaque flēre tua,
si tū mē, hospes, amās." Mīrō medicāmine corpus
　　ūnxit amātōrī, mīraque multa docet.　　　　　　　　　10
Nōn magnus labor inde bovēs adiungere magnōs;
　　illī flamma boum nūlla molesta fuit.
Parturiunt sulcī. Iam nascitur inde virōrum
　　turba armātōrum magna. Nec ille fugit.
Saxa iacit. Socium culpābat quisque, sed ensem　　　　15
　　strīnxit. Mox mīles mortuus omnis erat.
Sed malus ingentī custōdit corpore serpēns,
　　aurea nec quemquam vellera adīre sinit;
nam nōn clausa simul sunt omnia lūmina somnō:
　　quot dormīre oculī, tot vigilāre solent.　　　　　　　20
At quid nōn, Mēdēa, potes medicāmine? Mōlēs
　　serpentis somnō mox superāta iacet.

Aeētēs, -ae (*m*), King Aeëtes
crūdēlis, -is, -e, cruel
verbum, -ī (*n*), word
hērōs (the hero is Jason)
heu = **ēheu**
conticuit, (he) was silent
nec, and not
　　nec nōn, also
quae, and she
fīdus, -a, -um, faithful, trustworthy
5　**quod iubeō,** what I tell you
vīvus, -a, -um, alive
vellera (*n pl*), fleece
secūrus, -a, -um, without fear
dēbēbis, you will have to
multus, -a, -um, much
fleō, flēre (3), **flēvī, flētum,**
　　to lament over
mīrō medicāmine, with a strange
　　ointment
corpus . . . amātōrī, her lover's
　　body

10　**unguō, unguere** (3), **ūnxī, ūnctum,**
　　to smear
inde, after that, from there
adiungō, adiungere (3), **adiūnxī,**
　　adiūnctum, to yoke
boum, of the bulls
parturiunt sulcī, the furrows strain
　　to give birth
nascitur, is born
armātus, -a, -um, armed
15　**saxum, -ī** (*n*), a boulder
socium culpābat quisque, each
　　(of the armed men) began to
　　blame his neighbor
ensis, ensis (*m*), sword
malus, -a, -um, evil
nec quemquam sinit, and does not
　　allow anyone
lūmina, eyes
20　**quot . . . tot,** as many . . . so many
superātus, -a, -um, overcome

104

Answer in Latin or English the following questions on Versiculī 13 (Medea):

1. What was Jason's reaction to Aeetes' words (line 2)?
2. What word reveals the reason for this reaction?
3. What was the substance of these **crūdēlia verba** (see introductory paragraph)?
4. Why should Jason trust the words of Aeetes' daughter (see line 4 and introductory paragraph)?
5. Rewrite the Latin of lines 5–6 in English word order.
6. What does Medea ask Jason to do to prove his love for her (lines 7–9)?
7. In what ways did Medea help Jason (lines 9–10)?
8. What was the subsequent effect of this **medicāmen** (lines 11–12)?
9. What is the effect of the redundancy (anaphora) of **mīrus** in lines 9 and 10?
10. To whom or what does **illī** (line 12) refer?
11. What is the "crop" that the furrows strain to bear in line 13?
12. How does Jason react to this threat (lines 14–15)?
13. How does the situation resolve itself (lines 15–16)?
14. Of what poetic technique or device is **mox mīles mortuus** (line 16) an example? Find another example in this poem.
15. What is the effect of the placement of the words in line 17?
16. What do we learn about the dragon in lines 17–20?
17. Does **lūmina** (line 19) really mean "eyes"? Find its basic meaning in a Latin dictionary.
18. "Apostrophe" is a sudden break from the previous method of discourse and an address, in the second person, of some person or object, absent or present. Explain why line 21 is an apostrophe.
19. What do we learn about Medea from this apostrophe?
20. "Periphrasis" is a roundabout way of saying something. How else could you express the idea conveyed by **mōlēs serpentis** (lines 21–22)?
21. A particular sound can be used in poetry to create the effect of sleep. What is that sound and how is it effective in the last line of the poem?

FORMS

I. Nouns

Number / Case	1st Declension Fem.	2nd Declension Masc.	2nd Declension Masc.	2nd Declension Neut.	3rd Declension Masc.	3rd Declension Fem.	3rd Declension Neut.	4th Declension Fem.	4th Declension Neut.	5th Declension Masc.
Singular										
Nom.	puélla	sérvus	púer	báculum	páter	vōx	nōmen	mánus	génū	diēs
Gen.	puéllae	sérvī	púerī	báculī	pátris	vōcis	nōminis	mánūs	génūs	diḗī
Dat.	puéllae	sérvō	púerō	báculō	pátrī	vōcī	nōminī	mánuī	génū	diḗī
Acc.	puéllam	sérvum	púerum	báculum	pátrem	vōcem	nōmen	mánum	génū	diem
Abl.	puéllā	sérvō	púerō	báculō	pátre	vōce	nōmine	mánū	génū	diḗ
Plural										
Nom.	puéllae	sérvī	púerī	bácula	pátrēs	vōcēs	nōmina	mánūs	génua	diēs
Gen.	puellárum	servórum	puerórum	baculórum	pátrum	vōcum	nōminum	mánuum	génuum	diḗrum
Dat.	puéllīs	sérvīs	púerīs	báculīs	pátribus	vōcibus	nōminibus	mánibus	génibus	diḗbus
Acc.	puéllās	sérvōs	púerōs	bácula	pátrēs	vōcēs	nōmina	mánūs	génua	diēs
Abl.	puéllīs	sérvīs	púerīs	báculīs	pátribus	vōcibus	nōminibus	mánibus	génibus	diḗbus

II. Adjectives

Number	1st and 2nd Declension			3rd Declension		
Case	Masc.	Fem.	Neut.	Masc.	Fem.	Neut.
Singular						
Nominative	mágnus	mágna	mágnum	ómnis	ómnis	ómne
Genitive	mágnī	mágnae	mágnī	ómnis	ómnis	ómnis
Dative	mágnō	mágnae	mágnō	ómnī	ómnī	ómnī
Accusative	mágnum	mágnam	mágnum	ómnem	ómnem	ómne
Ablative	mágnō	mágnā	mágnō	ómnī	ómnī	ómnī
Plural						
Nominative	mágnī	mágnae	mágna	ómnēs	ómnēs	ómnia
Genitive	magnṓrum	magnā́rum	magnṓrum	ómnium	ómnium	ómnium
Dative	mágnīs	mágnīs	mágnīs	ómnibus	ómnibus	ómnibus
Accusative	mágnōs	mágnās	mágna	ómnēs	ómnēs	ómnia
Ablative	mágnīs	mágnīs	mágnīs	ómnibus	ómnibus	ómnibus

III. Numerical Adjectives or Numbers

Case	Masc.	Fem.	Neut.	Masc.	Fem.	Neut.	Masc.	Fem.	Neut.
Nominative	únus	úna	únum	dúo	dúae	dúo	trēs	trēs	tría
Genitive	úníus	úníus	úníus	duórum	duárum	duórum	tríum	tríum	tríum
Dative	únī	únī	únī	duóbus	duábus	duóbus	tríbus	tríbus	tríbus
Accusative	únum	únam	únum	dúōs	dúās	dúo	trēs	trēs	tría
Ablative	únō	únā	únō	duóbus	duábus	duóbus	tríbus	tríbus	tríbus

IV. Demonstrative Adjectives

Number / Case	Masc.	Fem.	Neut.	Masc.	Fem.	Neut.
Singular						
Nominative	hic	haec	hoc	ille	illa	illud
Genitive	húius	húius	húius	illíus	illíus	illíus
Dative	húic	húic	húic	illī	illī	illī
Accusative	hunc	hanc	hoc	illum	illam	illud
Ablative	hōc	hāc	hōc	illō	illā	illō
Plural						
Nominative	hī	hae	haec	illī	illae	illa
Genitive	hórum	hárum	hórum	illórum	illárum	illórum
Dative	hīs	hīs	hīs	illīs	illīs	illīs
Accusative	hōs	hās	haec	illōs	illās	illa
Ablative	hīs	hīs	hīs	illīs	illīs	illīs

V. Pronouns

Case	Singular					Plural				
	1st	2nd	3rd			1st	2nd	3rd		
			Masc.	Fem.	Neut.			Masc.	Fem.	Neut.
Nominative	égo	tū	is	éa	id	nōs	vōs	éī	éae	éa
Genitive			éius	éius	éius			eórum	eárum	eórum
Dative	míhi	tíbi	éī	éī	éī	nóbīs	vóbīs	éīs	éīs	éīs
Accusative	mē	tē	éum	éam	id	nōs	vōs	éōs	éās	éa
Ablative	mē	tē	éō	éā	éō	nóbīs	vóbīs	éīs	éīs	éīs

VI. Regular Verbs

			1st Conjugation	2nd Conjugation	3rd Conjugation		4th Conjugation
Present	Infinitive		paráre	habḗre	míttere	iácere (-iō)	audíre
	Imperative		párā	hábē	mítte	iáce	aúdī
			paráte	habḗte	míttite	iácite	audíte
	Singular	1	párō	hábeō	míttō	iáciō	aúdiō
		2	párās	hábēs	míttis	iácis	aúdīs
		3	párat	hábet	míttit	iácit	aúdit
	Plural	1	parámus	habḗmus	míttimus	iácimus	audímus
		2	parátis	habḗtis	míttitis	iácitis	audítis
		3	párant	hábent	míttunt	iáciunt	aúdiunt
Imperfect	Singular	1	parábam	habḗbam	mittḗbam	iaciḗbam	audiḗbam
		2	parábās	habḗbās	mittḗbās	iaciḗbās	audiḗbās
		3	parábat	habḗbat	mittḗbat	iaciḗbat	audiḗbat
	Plural	1	parābámus	habēbámus	mittēbámus	iaciēbámus	audiēbámus
		2	parābátis	habēbátis	mittēbátis	iaciēbátis	audiēbátis
		3	parábant	habḗbant	mittḗbant	iaciḗbant	audiḗbant

VI. Regular Verbs (continued)

			Infinitive	1st Conjugation	2nd Conjugation	3rd Conjugation		4th Conjugation
				parāre	habēre	mittere	iacere (-iō)	audīre
Future	Singular	1		parábō	habébō	míttam	iáciam	aúdiam
		2		parábis	habébis	míttēs	iáciēs	aúdiēs
		3		parábit	habébit	míttet	iáciet	aúdiet
	Plural	1		parábimus	habébimus	mittémus	iaciémus	audiémus
		2		parábitis	habébitis	mittétis	iaciétis	audiétis
		3		parábunt	habébunt	míttent	iácient	aúdient
Perfect	Singular	1		parávī	hábuī	mísī	iḗcī	audī́vī
		2		parávístī	habuístī	mīsístī	iēcístī	audīvístī
		3		parávit	hábuit	mísit	iḗcit	audī́vit
	Plural	1		parávimus	habúimus	mísimus	iḗcimus	audī́vimus
		2		parávistis	habuístis	mīsístis	iēcístis	audīvístis
		3		parāvḗrunt	habuḗrunt	mīsḗrunt	iēcḗrunt	audīvḗrunt

VI. Regular Verbs (continued)

		1st Conjugation	2nd Conjugation	3rd Conjugation		4th Conjugation
Infinitive		parāre	habēre	míttere	iácere (-iō)	audīre
Pluperfect Singular	1	parāveram	habúeram	míseram	iéceram	audīveram
	2	parāverās	habúerās	míserās	iécerās	audīverās
	3	parāverat	habúerat	míserat	iécerat	audīverat
Plural	1	parāverāmus	habuerāmus	miserāmus	iécerāmus	audīverāmus
	2	parāverātis	habuerātis	miserātis	iécerātis	audīverātis
	3	parāverant	habúerant	míserant	iécerant	audīverant
Future Perfect Singular	1	parāverō	habúerō	míserō	iécerō	audīverō
	2	parāveris	habúeris	míseris	iéceris	audīveris
	3	parāverit	habúerit	míserit	iécerit	audīverit
Plural	1	parāvérimus	habuérimus	mīsérimus	iécérimus	audīvérimus
	2	parāvéritis	habuéritis	mīséritis	iécéritis	audīvéritis
	3	parāverint	habúerint	míserint	iécerint	audīverint

VII. Irregular Verbs

			ésse	pósse	vélle	nólle	íre	férre
Present	Infinitive		ésse	pósse	vélle	nólle	íre	férre
	Imperative		es éste	— —	— —	nólī nólīte	ī íte	fer férte
	Singular	1	sum	póssum	vólō	nólō	éō	férō
		2	es	pótes	vīs	nōn vīs	īs	fers
		3	est	pótest	vult	nōn vult	it	fert
	Plural	1	súmus	póssumus	vólumus	nólumus	ímus	férimus
		2	éstis	potéstis	vúltis	nōn vúltis	ítis	fértis
		3	sunt	póssunt	vólunt	nólunt	éunt	férunt
Imperfect	*Singular*	1	éram	póteram	volébam	nōlébam	íbam	ferébam
		2	érās	póterās	volébās	nōlébās	íbās	ferébās
		3	érat	póterat	volébat	nōlébat	íbat	ferébat
	Plural	1	erámus	poterámus	volēbámus	nōlēbámus	ibámus	ferēbámus
		2	erátis	poterátis	volēbátis	nōlēbátis	ibátis	ferēbátis
		3	érant	póterant	volébant	nōlébant	íbant	ferébant
Future	*Singular*	1	érō	póterō	vólam	nólam	íbō	féram
		2	éris	póteris	vólēs	nólēs	íbis	férēs
		3	érit	póterit	vólet	nólet	íbit	féret
	Plural	1	érimus	potérimus	volémus	nōlémus	íbimus	ferémus
		2	éritis	potéritis	volétis	nōlétis	íbitis	ferétis
		3	érunt	póterunt	vólent	nólent	íbunt	férent

Note: perfect, pluperfect, and future perfect tenses are formed regularly from the perfect stem plus the regular endings.

Vocabulary

	ā or ab (+ *abl.*)	by, from
	ábeō, abíre (*irreg.*), ábiī, ábitum	to go away
24	abhínc	ago, previously
	ábsum, abésse (*irreg.*), áfuī	to be away, absent, be distant
	áccidit, accídere (3), áccidit	to happen
20	accúsō (1)	to accuse
	ad (+ *acc.*)	to, towards, at, near
	adhúc	still
18	ádiuvō, adiuváre (1), adiúvī, adiútum	to help
21	admóveō, admovére (2), admóvī, admótum	to move towards
18	ádsum, adésse (*irreg.*), ádfuī	to be present
	advéniō, adveníre (4), advénī, advéntum	to reach, arrive at
	advesperáscit, advesperáscere, advesperávit	to get dark
	aedifícium, -ī (*n*)	building
23	aedíficō (1)	to build
23	aéstus, -ūs (*m*)	heat
	Áge! Ágite!	Come on!
	áger, ágrī (*m*)	field
17	agnóscō, agnóscere (3), agnóvī, ágnitum	to recognize
	ágō, ágere (3), égī, áctum	to do, drive
	Quid ágis?	How are you?
26	albátus, -a, -um	white
24	áliquid	something
	álius, ália, áliud	other, another
	álter, áltera, álterum	the other, an other, a second
	ámbulō (1)	to walk
	amícus, -ī (*m*)	friend
	ámō (1)	to like, love
22	amphitheátrum, -ī (*n*)	amphitheater
	ancílla, -ae (*f*)	slave-woman
19	ánimus, -ī (*m*)	mind
20	ánimum recuperáre	to regain one's senses, be fully awake
19	in ánimō habére	to intend
19	ánteā	previously, before
25	antíquus, -a, -um	ancient
25	apériō, aperíre (4), apéruī, apértum	to open
	appáreō (2)	to appear
	appropínquō (1) (+ *dat.* or ad + *acc.*)	to approach, draw near (to)
22	áqua, -ae (*f*)	water
22	aquaedúctus, -ūs (*m*)	aqueduct

	árbor, árboris (f)	tree
23	árcus, -ūs (m)	arch
26	arēna, -ae (f)	arena, sand
	arrípiō, arrípere (3), arrípuī, arréptum	to grab hold of, snatch, seize
	ars, ártis (f)	skill
	ascéndō, ascéndere (3), ascéndī, ascénsum	to climb, go up
22	at	but
21	átque	and, also
25	átrium, -ī (n)	atrium, central room in a house
19	atténtē	attentively, closely
23	attónitus, -a, -um	astonished, astounded
	aúdiō (4)	to hear, listen to
24	aúreus, -a, -um	golden
	auríga, -ae (m)	charioteer
21	aúrum, -ī (n)	gold
	auxílium, -ī (n)	help

B

	báculum, -ī (n)	stick
21	béne	well
25	bóna, -ốrum (n pl)	goods, possessions
	bónus, -a, -um	good
	bōs, bóvis (m/f)	ox, cow
	brévis, -is, -e	short

C

	cádō, cádere (3), cécidī, cásum	to fall
	caélum, -ī (n)	sky
	cánis, cánis (m/f)	dog
21	captívus, -ī (m)	prisoner
24	cáput, cápitis (n)	head
17	caúda, -ae (f)	tail
	caúpō, caupốnis (m)	innkeeper
	caupốna, -ae (f)	inn
24	caúsa, -ae (f)	reason
	cáveō, cavếre (2), cávī, caútum	to watch out, be careful
26	cếdō, cếdere (3), céssī, céssum	to come, go
	celériter	quickly
	celérrimē	very fast, quickly
	cếlō (1)	to hide
18	cếna, -ae (f)	dinner
18	cếnō (1)	to dine, eat dinner
18	cértē	certainly
	céssō (1)	to be idle, do nothing, delay
	cíbus, -ī (m)	food
26	circếnsis, -is, -e	in the circus

116

23	circúmeō, circumíre (*irreg.*), circúmiī, circúmitum	to go around
22	Círcus, -ī (*m*)	Circus Maximus
	císium, -ī (*n*)	light two-wheeled carriage
	císta, -ae (*f*)	trunk, chest, box
	cívis, cívis (*m*)	citizen
	clámō (1)	to shout
	clámor, clāmóris (*m*)	shout, shouting
25	claúdō, claúdere (3), claúsī, claúsum	to shut
23	claúsus, -a, -um	shut, closed
24	clíēns, cliéntis (*m*)	client, dependent
20	cógitō (1)	to think
22	cólō, cólere (3), cóluī, cúltum	to cultivate
	commótus, -a, -um	moved
25	métū commótus	moved by fear, in a panic
22	condúcō, condúcere (3), condúxī, condúctum	to hire
20	conícíō, conícere (3), coniécī, coniéctum	to throw
22	cōnsídō, cōnsídere (3), cōnsédī	to sit down
	cōnspíciō, cōnspícere (3), cōnspéxī, cōnspéctum	to catch sight of
22	cōnstítuō, cōnstitúere (3), cōnstítuī, cōnstitútum	to decide
20	córpus, córporis (*n*)	body
	crās	tomorrow
	cubículum, -ī (*n*)	room, bedroom
18	cúbitum íre	to go to bed
18	cui	to whom, to him, to her
	cum (+ *abl.*)	with
21	cum	when
	cúnctī, -ae, -a	all
	Cūr . . . ?	Why . . . ?
22	Cúria, -ae (*f*)	Senate House
	cúrō (1)	to look after, attend to
	cúrrō, cúrrere (3), cucúrrī, cúrsum	to run
	custódiō (4)	to guard
25	cústōs, custódis (*m*)	guard

D

19	dē (+ *abl.*)	down from, concerning, about
	dēféssus, -a, -um	tired
	deínde	then, next
23	dēmónstrō (1)	to show
	dēscéndō, dēscéndere (3), dēscéndī, dēscénsum	to come or go down, climb down

117

	dēvértō, dēvértere (3), dēvértī, dēvérsum	to turn aside
19	dévorō (1)	to devour
19	dícō, dícere (3), díxī, díctum	to say, tell
	díēs, diḗī (m)	day
18	dīligénter	carefully
	discḗdō, discḗdere (3), discéssī, discéssum	to go away, depart
	díū	for a long time
21	dō, dáre, dédī, dátum	to give
24	dóceō, docḗre (2), dócuī, dóctum	to teach
17	dóleō (2)	to be sorry, sad
25	dómī	at home
	dómina, -ae (f)	mistress, lady of the house
	dóminus, -ī (m)	master, owner
22	dómō	out of the house
22	dómum	homeward, home
22	dómus, -ūs (f)	house
	dórmiō (4)	to sleep
	dū́cō, dū́cere (3), dū́xī, dúctum	to lead, take, bring
	dum	while, as long as
	dúo, dúae, dúo	two

E

	ē or ex (+ abl.)	from, out of
	Écce!	Look! Look at . . . !
	égo	I
	Éheu!	Alas!
24	Ého!	Hey!
20	éī	to him, her, it
21	éī, éae, éa	they
21	éīs	to them
	éius	his, her, its
24	émō, émere (3), ḗmī, ḗmptum	to buy
19	énim	for
	éō, íre (irreg.), ívī, ítum	to go
22	éō (adv.)	there, to that place
24	eórum	their
	éōs	them
	epístula, -ae (f)	letter
	équus, -ī (m)	horse
	érrō (1)	to wander, be mistaken
	ésse (see sum)	
19	Éstō!	All right!
18	ēsúriō (4)	to be hungry
	et	and
	étiam	also, even

	éum	him, it
	ex or ē (+ *abl.*)	from, out of
	excípiō, excípere (3), excépī, excéptum	to welcome, receive
24	excitátus, -a, -um	wakened, aroused
	éxcitō (1)	to rouse, wake (someone) up
	exclámō (1)	to exclaim, shout out
	éxeō, exíre (*irreg.*), éxiī, éxitum	to go out
18	éxplicō (1)	to explain
	exspéctō (1)	to look out for, wait for
22	éxstāns, exstántis	standing out, towering
17	exténdō, exténdere (3), exténdī, exténtum	to hold out
22	éxtrā (+ *acc.*)	outside
	éxtrahō, extráhere (3), extráxī, extráctum	to pull out, drag out

F

19	fábula, -ae (*f*)	story
	fáciō, fácere (3), fḗcī, fáctum	to make, do
	fátuus, -a, -um	stupid
26	fáveō, favḗre (2), fā́vī, faútum (+ *dat.*)	to favor, support
26	fēriátus, -a, -um	celebrating a holiday
	férō, férre (*irreg.*), túlī, látum	to carry, bring, bear
	ferṓciter	fiercely
	festínō (1)	to hurry
	fília, -ae (*f*)	daughter
	fílius, -ī (*m*)	son
20	fíniō (4)	to finish
	fortásse	perhaps
22	Fórum, -ī (*n*)	the Forum (town center of Rome)
	fóssa, -ae (*f*)	ditch
	fráter, frátris (*m*)	brother
	frū́strā	in vain
17	fúgiō, fúgere (3), fū́gī, fúgitum	to flee
	fúī (see sum)	

G

	gaúdeō, gaudḗre (2), gavī́sus sum	to be glad, rejoice
22	gaúdium, -ī (*n*)	joy
	gémō, gémere (3), gémuī, gémitum	to groan
25	gládius, -ī (*m*)	sword
25	gládium stríngere	to draw a sword
26	glṓria, -ae (*f*)	fame, glory
20	Graécia, -ae (*f*)	Greece
	Graécus, -a, -um	Greek

H

21	habḗnae, -árum (*f pl*)	reins
	hábeō (2)	to have, hold
	hábitō (1)	to live, dwell

	haéreō, haerḗre (2), haésī, haésum	to stick
19	héri	yesterday
17	hic, haec, hoc	this
	hīc (*adverb*)	here
	hódiē	today
17	hómō, hóminis (*m*)	man
22	hóminēs, hóminum (*m pl*)	people
	hṓra, -ae (*f*)	hour
	hórtus, -ī (*m*)	garden
17	hóspes, hóspitis (*m*)	friend, host, guest
22	hūc illū́c	here and there, this way and that
24	húıus	genitive of hic

I

25	iáceō (2)	to lie, be lying down
	iáciō, iácere (3), iḗcī, iáctum	to throw
	iam	now, already
	iánua, -ae (*f*)	door
	íbi	there
	id (see is)	
	idéntidem	again and again, repeatedly
	ígitur	therefore
	ignā́vus, -a, -um	cowardly, lazy
	ílle, ílla, íllud	that, he, she, it; that famous
22	illū́c	there, to that place
22	ímber, ímbris (*m*)	rain
21	ímmemor, immémoris	forgetful
	immṓbilis, -is, -e	motionless
26	immortā́lis, -is, -e	immortal
	in (+ *abl.*)	in, on
	in (+ *acc.*)	into
24	incéndō, incéndere (3), incéndī, incénsum	to burn, set on fire
	íncitō (1)	to spur on, urge on, drive
	índuō, indúere (3), índuī, indútum	to put on
	īnfírmus, -a, -um	weak, shaky
21	íngēns, ingéntis	huge
20	innocéntia, -ae (*f*)	innocence
	ínquit	(he, she) says, said
24	īnspíciō, īnspícere (3), īnspéxī, īnspéctum	to examine
22	intérdiū	during the day, by day
	intéreā	meanwhile
	interpéllō (1)	to interrupt
21	íntrā (+ *acc.*)	inside
	íntrō (1)	to enter, go in
	invéniō, invenī́re (4), invḗnī, invéntum	to come upon, find

120

20	invítus, -a, -um	unwilling, unwillingly
	ípse, ípsa, ípsum	-self, very
	īrátus, -a, -um	angry
	íre (see éō)	
	is, ea, id	he, she, it; this, that
	Íta vérō!	Yes!
	ítaque	and so, therefore
	íter, itíneris (n)	journey, road
	íterum	again, a second time
	iúbeō, iubḗre (2), iússī, iússum	to order, bid

L

23	lábor, labóris (m)	work, toil
	labṓrō (1)	to work
	lácrimō (1)	to weep, cry
	laétus, -a, -um	happy, glad
24	lápis, lápidis (m)	stone
17	látrāns, lātrántis	barking
24	lātrátus, -ūs (m)	a bark, barking
	látrō (1)	to bark
17	laúdō (1)	to praise
19	lávō, laváre (1), lávī, lavátum	to wash
22	lectíca, -ae (f)	litter
22	lectīcárius, -ī (m)	litter-bearer
18	léctus, -ī (m)	bed, couch
17	lēgátus, -ī (m)	envoy
	légō, légere (3), légī, léctum	to read
	léntē	slowly
23	líber, líbrī (m)	book
	líberī, -órum (m pl)	children
19	lícet, licḗre (2), lícuit	it is allowed
19	lícet nóbīs	we are allowed, we may
	lóngus, -a, -um	long
23	lúdī, -órum (m pl)	games
	lúpus, -ī (m)	wolf
25	lútum, -ī (n)	mud
20	lūx, lúcis (f)	light
20	príma lúce	at dawn

M

23	magníficus, -a, -um	magnificent
	mágnus, -a, -um	big, great, large, loud (voice)
21	mandátum -ī (n)	order, instruction
	máne	early in the day, in the morning
	máneō, manére (2), mánsī, mánsum	to remain, stay
17	mánus, -ūs (f)	hand
26	máppa, -ae (f)	napkin

121

	máter, mátris (f)	mother
22	máximus, -a, -um	very great, greatest, very large
	mē	me
19	médius, -a, -um	mid-, middle of
19	média nox	midnight
20	Mégara, -ae (f)	Megara (a city in Greece)
17	Mehércule!	By Hercules! Goodness me!
18	mélior, melióris	better
21	mercátor, mercātóris (m)	merchant
26	méta, -ae (f)	mark, goal, turning-post
25	métus, -ūs (m)	fear
	méus, -a, -um	my, mine
	míhi	for me, to me
19	míles, mílitis (m)	soldier
	Mínimē (vérō)!	Not at all! Not in the least! No!
22	mírus, -a, -um	wonderful, marvelous, strange
	míser, mísera, míserum	unhappy, miserable, wretched
	míttō, míttere (3), mísī, míssum	to send
17	módo	only
23	mólēs, mólis (f)	mass, huge bulk
	moléstus, -a, -um	troublesome, annoying
23	mōns, móntis (m)	mountain, hill
21	mónstrō (1)	to show
25	mors, mórtis, (f)	death
20	mórtuus, -a, -um	dead
	móveō, movére (2), mōvī, mótum	to move
	mox	soon, presently
26	múlier, mulíeris (f)	woman
	múltī, -ae, -a	many
22	multitúdō, multitúdinis (f)	crowd
22	múrus, -ī (m)	wall
21	mūs, múris (m)	mouse
	mússō (1)	to murmur, mutter

N

	nam	for
19	nārrátus, -a, -um	told
19	nárrō (1)	to tell (a story)
	-ne	(indicates a question)
	necésse	necessary
19	nécō (1)	to kill
	némō, néminis	no one
25	néque	and . . . not
	néque . . . néque	neither . . . nor
24	néque támen	but . . . not

	néscio (4)	to be ignorant, not know
	níhil	nothing
20	Níhil málī.	There is nothing wrong.
17	nísi	unless, if . . . not, except
	nóbīs	for us, to us
25	nóceō (2) (+ *dat.*)	to harm
	nócte	at night
21	noctúrnus, -a, -um	happening during the night
	nólō, nólle (*irreg.*), nóluī	to be unwilling, not to wish
	nómen, nóminis (*n*)	name
	nōn	not
	nóndum	not yet
18	Nónne . . . ?	(introduces a question that expects the answer "yes")
25	nōnnúmquam	sometimes
	nōs	we, us
24	nóster, nóstra, nóstrum	our
24	nóvus, -a, -um	new
	nox, nóctis (*f*)	night
	núllus, -a, -um	no, none
	númerus, -ī (*m*)	number
19	númquam	never
	nunc	now
	núntius, -ī (*m*)	messenger

O

20	obdórmiō (4)	to go to sleep
17	obésus, -a, -um	fat
23	occúrrō, occúrrere (3), occúrrī, occúrsum (+ *dat.*)	to meet
25	óculus, -ī (*m*)	eye
17	ólim	once (upon a time)
	ómnis, -is, -e	all, the whole, every, each
	ónus, óneris (*n*)	load, burden
24	oppréssus, -a, -um	crushed
19	óptimus, -a, -um	best, very good
19	Vir óptime!	Sir!
21	ōrátor, ōrātóris (*m*)	orator, speaker
17	os, óssis (*n*)	bone

P

23	Palātínus, -a, -um	belonging to the Palatine Hill
	parátus, -a, -um	ready, prepared
	párēns, paréntis (*m/f*)	parent
	párō (1)	to prepare
25	párvulus, -a, -um	small, little

	páter, pátris (*m*)	father
24	patrốnus, -ī (*m*)	patron
21	pátruus, -ī (*m*)	uncle
19	paulīsper	for a short time
21	pecűnia, -ae (*f*)	money
	per (+ *acc.*)	through, along
	perīculốsus, -a, -um	dangerous
	perículum, -ī (*n*)	danger
	pernóctō (1)	to spend the night
	pertérritus, -a, -um	frightened, terrified
24	pervéniō, pervenīre (4), pervḗnī, pervéntum	to arrive (at), reach
	pēs, péd̄ıs (*m*)	foot
	pétō, pétere (3), petīvī, petītum	to seek, look for, aim at, attack
	plaústrum, -ī (*n*)	wagon, cart
	plḗnus, -a, -um	full
22	plúit, plúere (3), plúit	it is raining
24	poḗta, -ae (*m*)	poet
	pốnō, pốnere (3), pốsuī, pốsitum	to put, place
21	pōns, póntis (*m*)	bridge
	pórta, -ae (*f*)	gate
	pórtō (1)	to carry
	póssum, pósse (*irreg.*), pótuī	to be able
19	post (+ *acc.*)	after
24	póstis, póstis (*m*)	door-post
19	póstquam	after
25	postrídiē	on the following day
17	(sḗ) praecipitā́re	to hurl oneself, rush
	praeclā́rus, -a, -um	distinguished, famous
17	praecúrrō, praecúrrere (3), praecúrrī, praecúrsum	to run ahead
21	praédō, praedốnis (*m*)	robber
26	prásinus, -a, -um	green
22	prīmum	first, at first
20	prīmus, -a, -um	first
20	prī́mā lū́ce	at dawn
	prī́nceps, prī́ncipis (*m*)	emperor
	prócul	in the distance, far off
	própe (+ *acc.*)	near
	puélla, -ae (*f*)	girl
	púer, púerī (*m*)	boy
19	pū́niō (4)	to punish
22	pū́rus, -a, -um	spotless, clean
Q 24	quadrā́tus, -a, -um	squared

	Quális . . . ?	What sort of . . . ?
	Quam . . . !	How . . . !
	Quam . . . ?	How . . . ?
	quámquam	although
20	Quándō . . . ?	When . . . ?
24	quās	which
23	quem	whom, which
24	Quī . . . ?	Who . . . ? (pl.)
	quī, quae, quod	who, which
	quídam, quaédam, quóddam	a certain
22	quíēs, quiétis (f)	rest
22	sē quiétī dáre	to rest
	quiéscō, quiéscere (3), quiévī, quiétum	to rest, keep quiet
	Quis . . . ? Quid . . . ?	Who . . . ? What . . . ?
17	Quid ágis?	How are you?
	Quō . . . ?	Where . . . to?
25	Quócum . . . ?	With whom . . . ?
	quod	because
	quod (see quī, quae, quod)	
	Quómodo . . . ?	In what way . . . ? How . . . ?
	quóque	also

R	raéda, -ae (f)	traveling carriage, coach
	raedárius, -ī (m)	coachman, driver
	rámus, -ī (m)	branch
21	rárō	seldom
20	recúperō (see ánimus)	
	rédeō, redíre (irreg.), rédiī, réditum	to return, go back
24	réditus, -ūs (m)	return
23	relínquō, relínquere (3), relíquī, relíctum	to leave
20	remóveō, removére (2), remóvī, remótum	to remove, move aside
	repéllō, repéllere (3), réppulī, repúlsum	to drive off, drive back
	reprehéndō, reprehéndere (3), reprehéndī, reprehénsum	to blame, scold
18	rēs, réī (f)	thing, matter, situation
18	rem explicáre	to explain the situation
	respóndeō, respondére (2), respóndī, respónsum	to reply
	révocō (1)	to recall, call back
	rídeō, rīdére (2), rísī, rísum	to laugh, smile
22	rīmósus, -a, -um	full of cracks, leaky
	rísus, -ūs (m)	laugh, smile
	rívus, -ī (m)	stream
	rógō (1)	to ask

125

	Rốma, -ae (f)	Rome
	Rōmắnus, -a, -um	Roman
26	russắtus, -a, -um	red
	rűsticus, -ī (m)	peasant

S

	saépe	often
	salűtō (1)	to greet, welcome
	Sálvē! Salvếte!	Greetings! Good morning! Hello!
22	sátis	enough
22	sátis témporis	enough time
	sceléstus, -a, -um	wicked
24	scíō (4)	to know
	scríbō, scríbere (3), scrípsī, scríptum	to write
	sē	himself, herself, oneself, itself, themselves
	sed	but
	sédeō, sedére (2), sḗdī, séssum	to sit
	sēmisómnus, -a, -um	half-asleep
	sémper	always
	senắtor, senātőris (m)	senator
	séptem	seven
	séptimus, -a, -um	seventh
21	sepúlcrum, -ī (n)	tomb
24	séquēns, sequéntis	following
20	sḗrō	late
25	sérvō (1)	to save
	sérvus, -ī (m)	slave
	sex	six
	sī	if
26	sígnum, -ī (n)	signal
	siléntium, -ī (n)	silence
	sílva, -ae (f)	woods, forest
	símul	together, at the same time
23	símulac	as soon as
20	símulō (1)	to pretend
25	síne (+ abl.)	without
	sóleō (2)	to be accustomed, in the habit of
	sollícitus, -a, -um	anxious, worried
	sólus, -a, -um	alone
20	sómnium, -ī (n)	dream
20	sómnus, -ī (m)	sleep
23	sónitus, -ūs (m)	sound
18	sórdidus, -a, -um	dirty
26	spectắtor, spectātőris (m)	spectator
	spéctō (1)	to watch, look at

	státim	immediately
20	stércus, stércoris (n)	dung, manure
24	stértō, stértere (3), stértuī	to snore
24	stílus, -ī (m)	pen
	stō, stáre (1), stétī, státum	to stand
	strḗnuē	strenuously, hard
22	strépitus, -ūs (m)	noise, clattering
25	stríngō, stríngere (3), strínxī, stríctum	to draw
22	stúltus, -a, -um	stupid, foolish
22	stúpeō (2)	to be amazed, gape
	sub (+ abl.)	under, beneath
	súbitō	suddenly
	sum, ésse (irreg.), fúī	to be
21	sū́mō, sū́mere (3), sū́mpsī, sū́mptum	to take. take up, pick out
20	súprā (adv.)	above, on top
22	súprā (+ acc.)	above
	súrgō, súrgere (3), surrḗxī, surréctum	to get up, rise
	súus, -a, -um	his, her, its, their (own)
	tabellárius, -ī (m)	courier
24	tabérna, -ae (f)	shop
	táceō (2)	to be quiet
22	tális, -is, -e	such, like this, of this kind
	támen	however, nevertheless
	tándem	at last, at length
	tántum	only
23	tántus, -a, -um	so great, such a big
	tē (see tū)	
	temerárius, -a, -um	rash, reckless, bold
	témpus, témporis (n)	time
	téneō (2)	to hold
25	térra, -ae (f)	earth, ground
21	térror, terrṓris (m)	terror, fear
18	tíbi	to you, for you
	tímeō (2)	to fear, be afraid of
	tóga, -ae (f)	toga
26	tótus, -a, -um	all, the whole
	trádō, trádere (3), trádidī, tráditum	to hand over
	tráhō, tráhere (3), tráxī, tráctum	to drag, pull
	trēs, trēs, tría	three
	tū (acc. tē)	you (sing.)
	túlī (see férō)	
	tum	at that moment, then
24	tumúltus, -ūs (m)	uproar, commotion
	túnica, -ae (f)	tunic

127

22	túrba, -ae (*f*)	crowd, mob
	túus, -a, -um	your (sing.)
U	Úbi . . . ?	Where . . . ?
	úbi	where, when
17	Únde . . . ?	Where . . . from?
22	úndique	on all sides, from all sides
	únus, -a, -um	one
	urbs, úrbis (*f*)	city
24	ut	as
	úxor, uxóris (*f*)	wife
V 18	váldē	very, exceedingly, very much
	Válē! Valéte!	Goodbye!
18	veheménter	very much, violently
	vehículum, -ī (*n*)	vehicle
	vélle (see vólō)	
26	vénetus, -a, -um	blue
	véniō, veníre (4), vénī, véntum	to come
	vérberō (1)	to beat, whip
24	verbósus, -a, -um	talkative
21	véster, véstra, véstrum	your (pl.)
25	vétō, vetáre (1), vétuī, vétitum	to forbid
	véxō (1)	to annoy
	vía, -ae (*f*)	road, street
	viátor, viātóris (*m*)	traveler
	vīcínus, -a, -um	neighboring, adjacent
26	víctor, victóris (*m*)	conqueror, victor
26	victória, -ae (*f*)	victory
	vídeō, vidére (2), vídī, vísum	to see
20	vidétur	he, she, it seems
19	vígilō (1)	to be watchful, stay awake
	vīlicus, -ī (*m*)	overseer, farm manager
	vílla, -ae (*f*)	farmhouse
24	vínum, -ī (*n*)	wine
	vir, vírī (*m*)	man
19	Vir óptime!	Sir!
	vírga, -ae (*f*)	stick
22	vísitō (1)	to visit
	vítō (1)	to avoid
23	vix	scarcely, with difficulty
18	vóbīs	to you, for you
	vólō, vélle (*irreg.*), vóluī	to wish, want, be willing
	vōs	you (pl.)
	vōx, vócis (*f*)	voice